Not all who wander are lost. But some people <u>are</u> lost. Very, very lost. And they like it that way. Thank you very much.

Dedicated to everyone who's ever had bank's charge them inexplicable fees, politicians manipulate their money, and stocks, houses, and gold crash around them.

R.R. Hauxley

FORWARD

This book is written with the bitcoin beginner and travel beginner in mind. This book contains broad analogies, sweeping generalizations, and keeps to a conversational tone. The humor is rather tongue-in-cheek as I seek to entertain while educating. You will no doubt find yourself wanting to know more about certain ideas, concepts, and tech. I wholeheartedly encourage further research. Try browsing Quora, Cointelegraph, Coindesk, Hackernoon, Zerohedge, Cryptomaniaks, and Googling other reliable sources of thought and news.

Disclaimer.
This book is a collection of stories from my travel journal as I traveled around the world. It is not intended to provide investment advice. This book should not be considered a solicitation, offer, or recommendation for the purchase or sale of bitcoin or other financial products and services discussed herein. You should not buy bitcoin or other cryptocurrencies unless you are prepared to sustain a total loss of the money you have invested plus any commission or other transaction charges. Moreover, certain names have been changed to protect people's privacy. Certain locations and dates have also been changed to protect privacy and in general artistic judgement. This book should be viewed as a collection of stories based on the truth, rather than the absolute truth. I've taken artistic liberties and embellished and even pulled from sheer fiction certain people, places, events, and stories. I've done this partly to entertain and partly because, quite frankly, my memory isn't what it used to be. Plus, I didn't always take the most detailed notes; what with constantly trying

to find safe places to sleep and clean food to eat.

Copyright © 2019 by RAFAEL HAUXLEY. All rights reserved worldwide (Earthwide, in this case), as well as galaxy-wide and, as far as it is possible, universe-wide. No part of this book may be reproduced or transmitted in any form or by any means without written permission from the author, except in the case of brief quotations embodied in critical articles and reviews -- and the occasional interpretive dance. Written permission can be obtained by writing to: thebitcointravelers@gmail.com

LOGBOOK. ENTRY 1.

T minus 2 days to launch.

On the black market...
My liver is worth: 55.78 bitcoins.
One of my kidneys: 16.41 bitcoins (if sold in China) and 4.11 bitcoins (if sold in India).
My skeleton: 0.99 Bitcoins -- spooky cheap.
My dick? Hm. I can't seem to find a reliable source for black market cocks.

That's not good.

Listen, say I get kidnapped -- which is entirely possible where I'm going. Then, after a few days of torture, the kidnappers say: "Deeply sorry about this, young man, but since no one came through with your ransom we'll need to go ahead and harvest one of your major organs -- have a preference?"

If the black market ran rife with naughty bits -- and my drinking habits still required a functioning liver -- I'd go ahead and have them lop off my cock.

sigh

Welcome, ladies and gentlemen, to my brain at 2 o'clock in the

morning. I can't stop thinking. I can't stop worrying. In a few very short days I fly away. Away from my family, my friends, the friendly neighborhood dog I pet on my way to work (Good old Charlie, with his lopsided ears and robber-scaring bark). In short -- away from everything I know. Away from home.
And for what?

To travel around the world ... on 1 bitcoin.

- A)   Beijing -- Bitcoin is banned. And I'm going during military prep for the 19th Congress of the Communist Party. Real solid timing on my part there.
- B)   Shanghai -- China's largest underground smuggling hub for opium, molly, cocaine, and black-tar heroin. Also -- I could be fined and jailed for jaywalking.
- C)   Hong Kong -- I can buy a fake Rolex for $10, or a real one that 'fell off the back of the truck' for $1500. Do they accept Bitcoin?
- D)   Burma (Myanmar)-- This is where shit hits the fan. There's a genocide boiling in NorthWest Burma. The Army is herding minorities and burning their villages. I've heard BTC helps them escape.
- E)   Cambodia -- Tourists are given the option to rent rocket launchers ... and blow up cows. Jesus Christ. Unreal. Are cryptocurrencies involved?
- F)   Bangkok -- The sex trafficking capital of S.E. Asia. Massage parlors, ping-pong shows, and "happy endings." Will this country be my happy ending? (Note to editor: delete that joke. I can do better).
- G) The Philippine's -- "President Rodrigo Duterte urges citizens to shoot drug addicts in the streets." He promised enough drug dealer bodies would be dumped in Manila Bay that fish there would grow fat from feeding on them. Does the same go for BTC traders?
- H)   India -- Transplant tourism. The Red Market. Hearts, lungs, livers handed off for a digital wallet full of crypto -- none of

which goes to the victims. Perhaps if I get desperate I'll sell a kidney.

I) Africa -- Not sure which country I'll wind up in. Not sure if I'll even make it. One bitcoin is not exactly a hefty sum. By this point I'll be running out -- and that's if the value of my single bitcoin hasn't buried it's two front teeth in the dirt.

J) Europe -- who am I kidding? The odds of me arriving in Europe with my wallet in one hand and my dick in the other are as tiny as both those things.

The goal: 365 days. 12 months. 1 year... on 1 bitcoin. To survive I'll need to couchsurf, eat cheap street food, and rely on the kindness of strangers -- cryptocurrency strangers.

If I accidentally trade my bitcoin for counterfeit money -- I'll go to foreign prison. If I get food poisoning -- I'll end up in a 3rd world hospital. If a couchsurfing host bails on me -- I'll be sleeping under a bridge. If I trade my bitcoin in a non-public place -- I'll get mugged. But if I trade in a public place I could be mistaken for a drug dealer -- and shot. In fact, I'll need to make a supremely concentrated effort to not get jailed, mugged, stranded, or shot. Jesus, no wonder I can't sleep. Why am I doing this?

2 WEEKS AGO.
A local Denny's Diner.
All-American breakfast.
A weekend routine for my father.

"Bitcoin is not money."
"Dad."
"Bitcoin will never be money."
"Dad."
"And you should shave off your beard."
"....It's a good beard, dad."

The waitress politely offers to refill his coffee. He waves her away. "You're mother keeps calling me. She used to never call me. I've worked hard to keep it that way. Now she's calling me day and night. Worried sick."
"She's a good mom."
"She's a pain in the ass. You're a pain in the ass. She calls me, telling me to talk you out of going, reading me headlines," he continues while salting his eggs aggressively, *"Jealous Gay Husband Uses Bitcoin to Hire Hitman. Sex trafficking on the Silk Road with Bitcoin. Terrorism on the rise with the rise of Bitcoin.* I'd hang up but she'd call me back with ten more."

"Not to worry, sheriff. I won't be financing a revolution."

"What will you be financing, hm? With this magic internet money?" He waves a breakfast sausage at the grocery store across the street. "Say I have a mind to go shopping. Fill the fridge. Put bread, butter, and beer on my table tonight. Think the teller will let me pay with your Facebook likes? Hm? Because that's what they are. These bitcoins, these junkie frequent flier miles. About as useful as condoms to the Pope."

I had to laugh at that one. "That's the spirit, sheriff. That's what I'll be traveling to find out. What the hell I can finance. What can I buy with my magic internet money."

"And how much of this fairy dust do you own?"
"One. I bought one Bitcoin."
"And how big a hole did it burn in your wallet?"
"Four thousand, seven hundred dollars…and change."
Dad's not the type to bulge his eyes out in surprise. His is the clench of the jaw that markes his disapproval. "You could have put that money toward getting your shit together."
I met his disapproval. "This is me getting my shit together."

"That a fact? And how much is your one pedobuck worth today?" he says, scrutinizing me over his cup of coffee. Waiting. He used to be a great cop. It's why I never could get away with anything as a kid. Still can't.
I look away. "Four thousand two hundred."

"Down five hundred bucks, already?"
"Yup."
"In one week?"
"Something like that."

Times like this. Right here. Times like this remind me of those unimaginative books where the author writes "and then he picked at his food." What a terrible line. Overused. Unimaginative. But here I am … picking at my food. No matter how old I get, dad's dis-

8

approval will always be something special.

"You know what you might have done with that money? Hm?" He tosses his used napkin on his empty breakfast plate. "Gone to a barber. Shaved your beard." Down went the last swig of his coffee. "Looked for another engineering job. Got another engineering job. Used that fancy university degree you're still in debt for."

"I've been trying."
"Try harder. Get your shit together."
"Sheriff, I -"
"Listen, my genius son, I will not bail you out. I will not let your mother bail you out. We do not have the money. What you are doing is a mistake. It will end in failure."
"Sheriff-"
"I am not finished. You have never taken a trip remotely like this in your entire life." He always had a remarkable way of raising his voice without actually raising his voice. "I will not be speaking ching-chong Chinese to some oriental dipshit deputy because you stuck your finger in someone's else's dumpling. Your mother will not fly out to Cambodia with a steaming bowl of chicken noodle soup because you ate tapeworm salad. And God forbid. God forbid you get taken, held for ransom, or sliced open."
"I understand."
"You do not understand." He begings ticking off fingers. "If you get stranded. If you get imprisoned. If you get hospitalized. If someone steals your magic computer fairy dust. Nobody will bail you out. There will be no cavalry. You will be on your own. Alone."
And now the silence. Silence like a large wave going out, giving you time to change your mind, time to rethink your life choices. Before the wave returns to knock your sandcastle out.
"No, Sherriff, I'm doing this."
"Why?"
"To find out if bitcoin is money. If it has a future."
"Unexceptable. Stick your nose in a book about it. Why do you want to go?"

"I've never done anything like this before. This'll test me. Make me grow."
"Pussy of a reason," he growls. "Why are you going?"
"I don't know. But I'll find out."
………..
….
After awhile he stands. "Remember." He takes out his wallet. "You get on that plane --- and there won't be no cavalry." Withdraws a few crisp bills. Tosses them on the table. "And only money … is money."

LOGBOOK ENTRY #3

T minus 0 days -- 10 minutes to launch.

Gate #2. Boarding of all non-priority passengers.

My phone rings. A picture of mom lights the screen.
"Hi mom."
"Be careful?" she says. "Please?"

I smile. She won't see it. She isn't one for video calls. But I'm sure she knows.
But there's something about airports and train stations. About leaving. It helps you say hard-to-say things. "I love you too, mom."

She takes a moment to be honest too. "You know dad loves you. He may not be proud of you. But he loves you."

Launch.

"Stop! Thief! That's my liver!"

Dear diary, I woke up shouting those words. Right in the center of a crowded airplane. Two hundred people bound for Beijing. A number of them are staring at me now. I am mortified. If I could find a parachute -- I would see myself out.
Instead I'm stuck on this flight for ten more bleary-eyed hours.

Right, nothing for it. Moving on. Now that I'm awake I should record a few of the dryer details regarding my journey: What is Bitcoin, how I plan to spend it, where I keep it safe, my backup plans in case shit goes sideways.

But before I begin I suppose I should jot down this dream -- the dream where I woke up shouting about my stolen liver. A friend of mine once claimed these things meant something. A glimpse into the future. Though if this dream was my future ...

On second thought, how about this: to help you crunch through the dry pages of this journal -- I'll save the good bits for last. Call it a bribe.

What is Bitcoin?

Is it money? Experts call it a cryptocurrency, keyword "currency." But my dad hammered down a solid argument: Only money ... is money.

If he can't use bitcoin to put bread, butter, and a cold frosty beer on the table ... what the hell is it good for anyway?

Therefore, according to the old sheriff, Bitcoin must not be money.

But what is money? Clams. Cheddar. Greenbacks. Benjamins. Cold hard cash. We earn it. We spend it. We sing about it, fight over it, fuck for it, and fuck up other people for more of it. "Money makes the world go 'round'" they say. And so it does. But what the hell is it?

Let's begin with the five mechanics of money. Then we'll see how Bitcoin stacks up. By the way, to aid me in explaining all this I'm going to go ahead and imagine you are sitting next to me. It so happens that the person actually sitting next to me on this flight is a little old Chinese grandma. She's got her elbows out. Taking up both armrests. This is you.

1) Divisibility. Money needs to split easily. So you're this won-

derful little old Chinese lady right here, right? Life in San Francisco is tough. English is too confusing and you're too old to care. But money is the universal language. So you take a crisp hundred dollar bill to the grocery store. A pack of your favorite smokes is eight dollars and fifty-two cents. It's gone up. What is the world coming to? But the siren call of nicotine beckons and you hand over the hundred. The teller, sick of this shit but smiling because this is America, counts out ninety-one dollars and forty-eight cents in change. You triple check it, or else he'll feel your wrath. All is well. The language of money has spoken. You waddle outside to light up -- only to find out you've forgotten your lighter.

The U.S. Dollar and all major currencies around the world are easily divisible. And, joy of joys, Bitcoin is too. In fact, Bitcoin can be divided far more than traditional cash. With cash you have $1.00 -- one dollar and two decimal places for change. One Bitcoin, on the other hand, contains eight decimal places (1.00000000). This means I could buy something for 0.00000001 Bitcoin. What I could buy with that, I have no idea....yet.

2) Portability. Money needs to be portable. After all, you're a frail, short old Chinese woman. If one U.S. dollar weighed as much as your dumpling-devouring grandson you'd be dead. Fortunately a dollar is very light and you can stuff wads of them for safe keeping into your wiry bra (After all, San Francisco is a dangerous place).

Money around the world is portable. Bitcoin even more so, being digital and thus not existing in the real world and all that jazz. For the purposes of my travels I've divided my 1 BTC into 3rds.

One third is stored on my Bitpay VISA card. The Bitpay VISA is a debit card run by the innovative folks at Bitpay. All I need to do is deposit some Bitcoin (in my case 0.33333 BTC) into my Bitpay account. Then my little slice of plastic here will work anywhere that VISA debit cards are accepted. I'll keep it tucked away in my wallet.

The second third of my bitcoin will be stored on my cell phone. I'll be using an app called Jaxx. It's a crypto wallet. It'll hold 0.33333 BTC. My plan here is to use it like a real world wallet. So let's say I find a unicorn -- in my case a restaurant or bar or hostel that accepts payment in BTC. To pay them I'll open up my Jaxx app, click 'send', scan their payment QR code, put in the amount, and away it goes.

My last third will remain firmly in my "oh shit" fund. This is the doomsday prepper stash. The "Shit hit the fan and clogged that motherf*cker" type of scenario. You see, if my wallet and Bitpay card get pickpocketed off me by some slick fingered fuck -- I'll still have my Jaxx mobile wallet on my phone. But if my wallet AND phone are both stolen what do I have? My 'oh shit' fund. My last third. My... aluminum block.

You see, Bitcoin can be stored offline. This is called 'cold storage.' To put it simply -- instead of storing the keys to my wallet online (Bitpay, Jaxx), I store them offline... by writing them down.

Most people write them down on paper. But to the best of my knowledge a piece of paper is flammable. Also if paper gets wet, such as when forgotten in a pocket in the washer, the paper turns into a soggy illegible mess. I've therefore taken the liberty of buying a small aluminum block -- which is waterproof and generally fireproof. I've engraved my BTC keys onto it. Afterwards I've strategically hidden said aluminum block in a ratty old sock. #genius.

3) Durability. Physical currency is fairly durable. Imagine your good fortune when, being an old chinese lady and hobbling back from the grocery with your cigs, you find a penny in the parking

lot. Slowly bending over so as not to displace a hip, you pick it up. It's from 1966. Wow. That's the year you became a mom. Times were tough back then. You could feed your whole family for a week on this penny. You tuck it away in your bra. Old habits die hard -- just like you. That penny is durable.

Bitcoin is also durable. I can send and receive Bitcoin over and over and it'll never wear out -- so long as computers and electricity exist.

4) Stability. Money requires stability. Imagine again that you speak Mandarin and look like Yoda. Yesterday you bought ingredients for your world famous chicken feet soup. A whole bushel of feet cost two dollars. A fair price. But imagine if, by the time you trundled to the check out stand, they cost twenty dollars. Then when the checkout boy rang them up they cost a quarter. You pull money out of your bra and they're back up -- to three hundred dollars -- only to nose-dive to half a penny. You'd have some strong words flying out your yapper. All in mandarin too, no doubt. Just a foaming cup of foreign grandma. The boy would be petrified. Poor thing.

Money needs to be stable. Unfortunately this is where Bitcoin begins to break down. My single bitcoin set me back a grand total of $4,724. Just before I boarded this flight I nervously checked the price. $4,822. Alright. It's up. Maybe I can afford an in-flight beer. But no. What if by the time I land this Bitcoin is down to $3,000? It's entirely possible. It's happened before. Just a few months ago in April it tanked 30%. In one week. That's as bad as someone stealing my phone with one-third of my money on it.
Now I'll be traveling on 1 bitcoin. Will it perform like regular money and slowly, equally drain away? Or will I be buying an airplane ticket one day and the next day spending the exact same amount on a bushel of chicken feet?

Bitcoin is not stable. It is volatile. Exceedingly volatile. Billionaire Mark Cuban proclaimed bitcoin was a bubble about to pop.

Any day now. Pop. Straight to zero.

On the other hand, cyber security leader John McAfee tweeted that a single bitcoin would hit $500,000. In fact, he believes in the epic rise of bitcoin with such conviction that he added: "if not -- I'll eat my dick on national television." Bold statement there, John. For your sake -- and mine -- I hope bitcoin continues to go up and you get to keep your bait and tackle.

5) Acceptability. Money must be accepted by people. It could be clams, bones, cheddar, pooka shells, or at one point for the ancient Babylonians -- human skulls. If it's accepted by people, then people will earn it, spend it, sing about it, and suck back alley dick for it. But if no one accepts it -- well like my old sheriff said -- it's about as useful as condoms to the Pope.

Money must be accepted by people. This is the foundation; The foundation upon which my dad's argument is built; The foundation upon which everyone who questions, slanders, or mocks Bitcoin builds their logic. If Bitcoin is not accepted -- it is not money.

But hold the damn phone.

Several hours ago the flight attendant pushed a cart down my aisle. He politely offered a cup of lukewarm tea. I asked for alcohol. He said that would be five dollars. I remembered seeing an old fiver leftover in my wallet. Better spend it before I can't anymore. Going to China and all. And then it struck me.

I'm flying to a nation of one billion three hundred million people. That's over four times as many people as the United States. For every red blooded, whistling Dixie American who would gladly accept my money -- four other people would not. My money will be no good in China.

Sure they'd understand my five American dollars are valuable.

They'd agree it was divisible, portable, durable, and stable. But accepted? No, not everyone is a walking money-exchange with the latest currency conversions rolling through their head. They wouldn't know if my five dollars is worth a hot meal and a bubble bath -- or a cold squid in a plastic bag. They don't know. They'd laugh and politely tell me the mandarin equivalent of "hit the road, dumbass."

Come to think on it, it's the same in the states. Say you take a once-in-a-lifetime trip to London, Paris, and Rome. After returning you find a few loose British Pounds and a handful of Euro's in your pocket. These are major world currencies. They are, without a doubt, money. When in Rome, you bought a ticket to the Colosseum. In Paris -- a lemon meringue tart. In London -- a flimsy umbrella. But as soon as you return stateside and waltz into Starbucks -- you can't buy a muffin. American's will not accept the British Pound Sterling or the Euro -- and vice versa.

I'm coming around to the opinion that "acceptability" as a foundational principle of money is very much relative. And if money is all relative --- then can bitcoin be money?

I suppose we'll find out.

Time for some shut-eye. The little Chinese grandma next to me is already fast asleep. Amazing how such a tiny, frail old thing can snore louder than a tractor in heat. Hopefully I won't wake her again by yelling about thieves stealing my internal organs.
Ah. Right. I promised an explanation of that unfortunate incident. Here it is:

A monkey stole my liver.

It wore billowy yellow pants, a jaunty red fez, and just before it nicked my 'organic alcohol processing unit,' it spoke in a sincerely terrible british accent: "Ya don't deserve 'em. There's better men out there what deserve 'em more."

Just a real asshole of a monkey.

I have no other context. It's all faded now. Where I was, how I got there, why the monkey had to be so mean. No idea. I'll leave it for the psychologists.

DAY 1

Beijing - China.

BTC remaining: 1.00000000 -- Net Worth: $4,644

First impression: I'm far from home. I am so very far from home. I've been away from home before. Visits to distant family. Small adventures. Never like this though. Never to a place that feels this … foreign.

Chinese letters surround me. Giving me directions to god knows where. Advertising to me god knows what (Is that a bar of soap on that billboard or a candy bar?). All in a language I can't read. A language I've only ever seen tattooed on the back of a fat hookers ass. She said it meant 'strength.' I think I just passed the same symbol above a sticky noodle cart.

Food carts and stands hold street corners. They're holding the city together. Serving fried white rice, fried yellow noodles, fried off-green vegetables. Without these food stands the city would fall apart. It's the fumes. The fried oil wafts into the air. It mixes with oily diesel. It churns with concrete dust from mushrooming highrises. It wafts on the heat and noise of rush hour traffic. Sticking to buildings. Coating windows. Filling cracks and crevices. This is the glue of modern industrial China. If I breathe it in long enough, I'll get stuck here too.

Perhaps that's why all these people are here. All around me. They're stuck here. Busy. They're all so god damn busy. I've been to Los Angeles and I've seen New York. I remember thinking "this is a beehive. I'm in the middle of an overworked beehive." But China, Beijing, is no beehive. A beehive drips with honey. It glitters in sugar gold. This city is a termite hill.

I've nothing against termites. They give me the impression of ants with engineering degrees. Ants will build small mounds of dirt. They burrow tunnels and shuffle dirt around. Termites construct skyscrapers. They reach for the sky using just sand and their own spit. Marvelous.

At the same time, though, a termite hill is nothing decorative. It's grey concrete. Utilitarian. Expressionless. And the same must be said of Beijing, or at least the majority of it. This is a city for the worker. The day laborer. The 9-to-9 man pulling 12 hour shifts to feed his family.

But look at me getting all pretentious and philosophical. What the hell do I know anyway. I've only been here for one day.

DAY 3

Beijing - China.

BTC remaining: 0.97 -- Net Worth: $4,390

Steady as she goes. Bitcoin's holding the line. It's fluctuating between $4,400 and $4,600. My Bitpay VISA is doing its job. It's allowing me to buy food and, far more important to my health and general wellbeing: cheap alcohol. I need it to disinfect my insides after the food around here. It's not that I'm cheap -- I'm also curious. What do the locals scarf down on a daily basis in this city? Is it tasty? Is it edible?

To find the answer I walked to restaruants with a complete lack of tourists; places where the look I got was "What the fuck are you doing here?"

One thing's certain: DO NOT read the labels before ordering your food. Go by the picture. Does the picture look scrumptious? Skip the label. Order the damn food. You see, for some reason Chinese people love translating everything into English. No one spell checks it. No one checks if it even makes sense. Perhaps they enjoy the way english words look -- in much the same way certain white people want tattoos of Chinese characters that say 'only the brave' but instead mean 'stick of unsalted butter.'

Case in point: I popped into a restaurant yesterday -- the kind with laminated menus. I took pictures:

A plate of pan-fried shrimp -- **"Seafood family photo."**

A seasoned bowl of yellow noodles -- **"Chinese caterpillar fungus loofah mix."**

One bowl of steaming clam chowder -- **"Cooked bacterial fish rot."**

And my all time favorite: wide egg noodles --- **"Old man's skin."**

Mark me down for scared AND hungry. Being an amateur tourist with an amateur digestive tract -- who has yet to experience 'the traveler's two-step' -- I ordered all the above. The shrimp were indeed succulent, the yellow noodles seasoned sensationally, the clam chowder hot and fresh, and the egg noodles would make Anthony Bourdain proud. That said, I'm never going back. The entire time I ate ... my imagination interrupted.

A bite of "Seafood Family Photo" had me asking -- did I just eat the dad or mom? Maybe one of the kids? Timmy? Did I just wolf down poor overcooked Timmy? You monster.

A bite of "Chinese caterpillar fungus loofah mix" had me imagining if this is what a caterpillar would taste like. Or a loofah, like the one in my ex's shower, it'd taste just like this.

"Cooked bacterial fish rot." I couldn't stop wondering if, maybe, it would be good for me? You know, because of the bacteria. Like a probiotic. Like yogurt. I'm eating fish yogurt right now. Amazing. No don't spit it out! This is what being a tourist is all about! Coward.

"Old man's skin." Oh. Oh god. Dear god. Dear lord who art in heaven. This is exactly. Yeah. This is exactly Old Man's Skin. Slimy. Stringy. Slurpy. This is what the devil serves in hell. Why did I order this? I will remember this. Mark my words. This'll ruin noodles for the rest of my life. My taste buds are telling me it's good but fuck me for reading the label.....Hey do you think this is what happens to old people who pass away in retirement homes? They're made into these noodles?

There we go. That's the image. That's the image to make me puuush that bowl away. Push it away real good.

No surprise I walked out and went hunting for bottles of cheap beer. Problem is I can't find beer with an ABV above 3%. I could get a buzz faster by leaving grapes out to rot. Not to worry though, I've found Baijiu. It's Eastern moonshine. Red Dragon's Piss. Chemically distilled rice alcohol. 80 proof. The bottle has a flammable warning on it. No wonder. This stuff tastes like my last relationship -- toxic.

I'm stretching my Bitcoin and gathering experiences from more than strange foods and strange drink though. I'm staying with strangers too. I'm couchsurfing.

Couchsurfing. The staple of traveling on a shoestring while meeting the world. Not that it's all five-star rooms with flower scented toiletries. Finding a couchsurfing host takes time and personalized emails. Send out, say, fifty or so requests over several days and someone opens their door.

After all that's what couchsurfing is: opening your door, opening your home, to a stranger. Granted, the whole system allows for reviews and pictures and emailing back-and-forth -- hopefully giving each person enough info on whether or not the other person is an axe-wielding murderer, or worse, someone who doesn't do their dishes.

Yet for the adventurous -- who know the meaning of 'polite as a pilgrim' -- couchsurfing is seeing the world as it truly is -- through the eyes of a local.

Stolen Wallets

My host's name is LeBron Chu. His first name isn't exactly LeBron -- it's something remarkably unpronounceable for me (a Chinese character that looks like a house on fire).

He's a mechanical engineer by day and an absolute basketball fanatic by night. He tells me that if he could be anyone living or dead he'd be LeBron James. I could see it. Not in the way he looks, maybe -- he's got the height and shape of a traffic cone. But man, if his personality could play ball -- he'd fly cross-court dunking hoops with camera lights poppin.

His biggest dream is to go see a real American basketball game; he wouldn't even care if he sat in the nosebleeds, as long as he got to be there, paint his face, wear a big poofy colored wig, and cheer using a foam finger. "LeBron number one!"

This bonded us because my first emails to him (while looking for hosts) were personalized with my time playing basketball (I neglected to mention it was middle school). Yes, I was a real dunkmaster back then. Settling scores on court. It was easy back then. The hoops were so short teachers often mistook them for trash bins.

Lebron's pad is shockingly small, or perhaps the polite word is "efficient." It's one room. To the left is a "kitchen" -- a minifridge with a single burner on top. To the right is the bathroom -- which couldn't fit the real LeBron's left foot. The sink is built onto the top of the toilet tank -- when I rinse my hands the water flows into the toilet tank for later flushings. Above the toilet is the showerhead. Taking a shower requires closing the toilet lid and standing around the toilet like a cowboy straddling a horse. Straight ahead is his bunk bed. He sleeps at the top. The lower area is reserved for his desk, computer covered with stickers, and a chair made of two plastic beer bins. Yet despite this cramped living space -- LeBron fills it with life. His life.

Poster's drap the walls. Kobe Bryant, Karl "The Mailman" Malone, John Stockton. He loves the Utah Jazz in particular. Given cities to visit in America he answers "Hollywood, New York, and Salt Lake City."

His love for the sport began when he was little, watching the Jazz play. He happily shows off his most prized possession: an official NBA basketball. He tells me he paid to have it shipped "aaallll the way from USA." I murmur in admiration and politely keep quiet about the "Made in China" sticker -- probably affixed to this ball not far from here. Ironic.

As for me, I sleep on a cot. My legs in the kitchen and my head in the entry. But hey, LeBron's pad is a stroll from major tourist spots. Maybe that's why I keep seeing petite Chinese girls standing at apartment corners -- wearing provocative outfits. Prostitutes for the tourists? I wonder if they accept BTC.

Anyway, in the last few days LeBron's joined me to wander around a few fascinating places -- for which he shared many amusing facts.

Amusing fact #1: Royal cats guard the Forbidden City.

Descended from ancient royal breeds, these cats prowl the labyrinth of this historic palace, terminating vermin and keeping company to ghosts.

Amusing fact #2: Ancient Emperors employed a royal armpit sniffer.

The armpit sniffers job ensured the emperor would always be wafting his best with each salut.

Amusing fact #3: No one could see the emperor -- and live.

Obviously a chosen few were allowed to see the man -- however most people were not. To ensure no one even caught a sneak-peak -- whenever the emperor would travel outside the Forbidden City a marching band would travel ahead. They rung bells if the emperor chose to turn left and pound drums if he'd be turning right. Traveling straight would be announced by both bells and drums. A big loud parade -- you were forbidden to watch.

Amusing fact #4: Emperors would have harems -- often with dozens even hundreds of women.

The emperor's sex schedule would be meticulously planned out by royal staff. He would be given only the best, most fertile and eligible women during peak cycles of the moon and stars. On his off time he was allowed to have "consorts" -- male sexual partners -- if he so wished.

Amusing fact #5: The current President of China banned Bitcoin.

Wait. That's not amusing at all.

But, apparently, that is the reason LeBron chose to host me. He wants to learn about Bitcoin. He first heard about it a few weeks ago. The 19th Communist Congress has been trumpeting itself across the news. Big wigs from all around the country will meet in Beijing.

President Xi Jinping is preparing for re-election. To show his power and unfaltering stance against corruption -- he banned ICO's, Bitcoin exchanges, and for all intents and purposes -- banned Bitcoin. Naturally this peaked LeBron's curiosity. In his words: "if my government is against it -- maybe I will try it."

Ah, LeBron, you traffic cone shaped anarchist. I like the way you think.

When it comes to freedom, especially from governmental oppression, he's endlessly curious. That curiosity is born from a life under the ever watching eyes and corrupt claws of the Great River

Crab (apparently the Chinese slang for Big Brother). During one of our sightseeing expeditions he gave an example by pointing at the sky -- a dystopian smog gray.

"Soon," he said with a wry grin, "blue sky. APEC blue."
"APEC blue?"
"Fake."
"How? How do they fake a blue sky?"
"Easy. Jinping's Party. They show power. Order shut down for big factories, deep fry restaurants. Also, place where -- places where dead bodies burn?"
"Cremation."
"Also closing. Makes perfect blue sky."

Damn. A blue sky out of this peasoup of pollution. Out of these stacks of dull concrete apartments cut by highways of angry drivers. All choking on the secondhand smoke of factories, fry kettles, and crematoriums. A blue sky would be a welcome sight. Then again, the fact it was made by their government -- all to impress a handful of politicians stumbling in for a week of rigged elections -- had me wonder if I was strolling the grounds of a giant political prison.

"And now they want to ban Bitcoin?" I ask.
"Yes."
"Why?"

"I also want to know why," he said, meeting my eyes. "I need to know why." He then went on to drop a few truths; Things I could tell he'd been thinking about for a long time. "In China our government gives big names to itself. Names to make us believe they work for us. Names to make us believe they care about us. Us, the people. Always the people. They say -- *People's* Bank of China. Supreme *People's* Court. National *People's* Congress. My country. Do you know the name of my country? It is not China. It is not only just China. My country is the *People's* Republic of China."

That gave me pause for thought.

He lowered his voice. "My parents believe them. Believe they will grow China, will make us powerful. Believe government will help people, protect people. But I do not believe."

"Why do you not believe?"
In the blink of an eye he whipped out his phone. "I am not free. They watch all I do. All I say -- on WeChat -- they know. They know where I am. Right now. All the time." He shoved the phone back in his pocket.

"I feel like a child but they are not my parents. Parents want children to grow up, to think for themselves, to be adults, to be free. But this government is not like good parents. They are bullies, bullies who want to control people; Tell people what to do, what to say, how to think. Control. They want to control me." He paused to breath.

"Now they ban Bitcoin. I only hear about Bitcoin two weeks ago -- already they want to ban it. Before people learn… they ban. Why? Maybe it is bad for me. Maybe bad for people." He gave one of those exaggerated shrugs people give when they're worked up. "I want to find out, before they take it away."

I stood in silence. He'd handed over several heavy thoughts. Perhaps my struggle with their weight made him realize their gravity too.

He tried to diffuse the tension with a laugh. "Don't repeat. They take me to prison." Another forced laugh. "Chinese prison very bad. No internet, haha." He kept trying to laugh it off.

I only believed him more.

DAY 7

Beijing - China.

BTC remaining: 0.944 -- Net Worth: $2,992

Well shit. It's happening. Bitcoin is crashing. The bubbling is popping. I just lost a thousand dollars. In one day. Snap of the fingers. Blink of an eye. From $4,xxx to $3,xxx in a day. Gone.

Yesterday I could cash out and buy a shitty car. Today I could cash out and buy a much shittier car -- the kind you get at a police auction because the meth heads didn't want it.

At this rate my organ-stealing kidnappers won't need to pull me into their van. I'll find their van myself. Offer up my organs. Here you go. Dig in boys. Just pay me enough to get me home. And my liver. Leave me my liver. I'll need it. My plan for post-op back-of-the-van surgery is drowning myself in a few barrels of Red Dragon Piss.

Mmmm, major organ failure never tasted so good.

DAY 8

Beijing - China.
BTC remaining: 0.944 -- Net Worth: $3,522

Jesus tap-dancing Christ, I have whiplash.

The price of Bitcoin rebounded with force. It's back above the waterline. No need to find a rusty van. I'm keeping my insides.

But holy hell. I suspected Bitcoin's volatility would be a roller-coaster -- but this is bungee jumping off the Empire State while blindfolded.

I jump off and then wonder ... am I going to bounce back up? Or will they be digging my two front teeth out of the dirt? I don't know! And no one will tell me because they're all bungee jumping blindfolded next to me, screaming their little minds out. How do those wolves on Wall Street deal with this stress? Hm? Lines of coke and jerking off?
Bitcoin needs to hold from here. Fingers crossed. Otherwise I'll need to take a page from the wolves of Wall Street and invest in hand lotion.

DAY 14

Beijing - China.
BTC remaining: 0.872 -- Net Worth: $4,544

Hm. My BTC wallet is getting thinner but my net worth is growing. I could get used to this.

These will be my last few days in Beijing. What a ride. Today, LeBron and I are wandering over to the Beijing Bitcoin Association meetup.

The meetup is announced on meetup.com and open to all. Though I must say -- the description raises a few curiosities.

> *"We're keeping this a lower profile event than normal given the sensitivity in Beijing during the Party Conference."*

Excellent. Politics and intrigue and Bitcoin. This should prove enlightening.

---We attended the meetup. This is how it went down---

Location: Jing-A taproom. A microbrew pub. In a city of 22 million people there's bound to be a handful of recovering AA members who need a cold one.

The place is easy to picture. Once you've seen one brewpub you've seen them all. Dim mood lighting to make people look better; bartenders with rolled up sleeves showing off overpriced ink; a beer board of 'punny' names: Circum Session Ale, Smooth Hoperator, Audrey Hopburn, Hoppy Ending, Hopitmus Prime.

It's a beer for god's sake. All I need to know is the ABV. Is it above 6%? Because I need to get socially lubed up. Lubed up enough to handle all the unvaccinated small talk soon to be inserted in my ear canal.

I saddled up to the bar and ordered an IPA. This one boasts quite the title: Airpocalypse, Double IPA, Beyond Index. The bartender tells me it's not on discount today, unfortunately, due to the excellent air quality.

"What?"

He proceeds to enlighten me. Beijing tends to be heavily polluted. Due to this (and as a clever marketing ploy) JING-A decided to brew the Airpocalypse. When smog is thick enough to choke on --- the beer is cheap. When the air is crystal -- the beer is the most expensive in the bar. And today, on account of clear APEC blue sky's thanks to the 19th communist congress, it's the most expensive it's ever been.
God I hate communism.

Nevertheless this double IPA is also the strongest beer on tap. 8.8%. And since my BTC pumped my networth up … I'm taking the beer.

LeBron, on the other hand, declines. He points to his cheeks, tells me beer turns them redder than the Chicago Bulls, and reminds me about the bitcoin meetup.

Right. And now, with a pint of social lub, we search for the meetup.

The bar is packed. From door knobs to barstools -- a sea of drunken expats. Germans, Brits, Australians -- the same white face copy/pasted. Each one nursing their 'Western style beer' and commiserating about the hard knocks of life in a foreign country. I'm just another camel at the local oasis.

Then a few bitcoin buzzwords leap into my ears from the left.

"Segwit2x fork in November."
"Transaction volume milestone."
"ASIC boost."
"Bitmain 51% attack."

"Hey folks," I interrupt, "is this the Bitcoin meetup?"

All talk stops.
This puts my eyebrows up. I've been to many a meetup. None this high strung.

The group is a handful of guys in their mid-thirties. One older gentleman. Most of them sport t-shirts and jeans. A few wear the blue collar business attire of the Western working stiff. Everyone holds a frosted mug of beer (well, except for the old guy. His is a glass of water). They glance at LeBron and me. Something like suspicion seems to narrow their eyes -- or am I seeing things?

"Yeah welcome," says one of the bros, breaking the tension. "Yeah this is the BTC meetup. Where you from?"

Small talk ensues. A necessary gambit. It goes something like: I'm from Portland. Yeah the place with the hipsters. And the beards. Right. And Starbucks. Yup. Loads of salmon. Sure are. Smoked? No I've never smoked my salmon. I know, it's a pity. No, I don't own a Tesla. Right. Beautiful cars. Yes. I should have bought Bitcoin seven years ago. Then I could buy a Tesla. I could buy the whole fucking factory now."

Soon, however, LeBron struck to the heart of the matter.

"Why is my country banning Bitcoin?" he asked, searching their faces for answers.

Surprisingly most of the guys turned away. Perhaps unwilling to discuss politics? Only one kid met us with an answer: Jack. Young-ish chap, as most people in bitcoin seem to be. Asian too, like LeBron. But that's where the similarities stopped. Where LeBron dressed in baggy, student-budget clothes -- Jack wore tight, loud, clothes: a blue button up shirt and designer jeans. Jack struck a handshake firm as a Western insurance salesman.
"We are a threat to China!" Jack announced. "Bitcoin is a threat to China," he tells us straight off the cuff. "To the banking system, to the government, to the president."

"Why?" presses LeBron.

"Cause it makes people rich!" Jack answers, lifting his beer high. "I bought BTC back in 2015 for guess how much. Go on. Throw a dart at it. Guess!" His grin jumps between us.

LeBron shrugs helplessly.

"$400!" crows the kid. "I've 10x'ed my money. I'm six figures now, baby! Going to the moon! Gonna get me a lambo. Banana yellow. Like the banana hammock I'll wear at nudist beaches. Lambo to the moon! That's the beauty. That's the genius. It's making people" he stresses his next words *"independently wealthy."* The grin turns serious. "No more banks. No more loans. No more government taxes. They can't trace my bitcoin. They can't take my bitcoin! It's mine!"

34

I'm half expecting this guy to follow up with his best Gollum impression.
LeBron, somewhat dazed by the sales tactics, can only ask "how?"
"Decentralization, amigo!" Jack fires back. He then fires off a few more rounds from his buzzword cannon. "The Bitcoin blockchain. Its this immutable, trustless ledger. It's a triple ledger. Permissionless, transparent, immutable, decentralized blockchain."

LeBron brain is shot full of holes. "What?"

The question sails right by Jack. He takes a swig of his stout. "How much you got?"

"What?"

"Bitcoin! How much? Now I'm no whale -- That's 1,000 BTC. I'm more like an octopus. Ya know. 47 BTC. Right here. Octopus level. Tryin to be a dolphin though!"
"Dolphin?" murmurs LeBron in mounting confusion. "No, nothing. I have nothing."

Jack, noticing LeBron has nothing to offer shifts all his attention to me. "How about you, amigo? You bought some, right?"

"Uh yeah. One."
"One. Alright alright. That's shrimp level. Good start. Good start. Time to buy more."
"No, just one for now."

"Whaaaaaaat? Why, buddy? You gotta get that bread, amigo!"
"I'm traveling on it. Around the world for one year ... on one bitcoin."
Jack put down his beer -- his version of a jaw drop. "Bro, shut the fuck uuuuppp! That is raaaad. The bitcoin cryptoshere is amaaaaaazing. Go to one of those after-parties. Tits! Just tits! Everywhere your dick points. Cornucopia of tits. Big, small, lopsided,

all sortsa tits. Pizza nippled tits. Beer flavored tits. It's the good life. Sweeeeet life!"

"………."

"Here take my Telegram info," he pressures, until I take out my phone, download Telegram (a messaging app of some sort), and add him. "If you need anything! Aaaaannnyyything. Like aa-aannyyythiiiiiiiiiiiiiiiiiiiiiiiiing -- tell me! I know people." He proudly nods with lidded eyes and pursed lips like a #realOG. "And people know ME."

I politely give him a couple finger guns.

He picks up his beer like the long-missed pacifier it is. "So when'd you start this bigass tour?"

"Couple weeks ago."

"Damn you still a *shrimp shrimp*, haha. Where you off to?"

"Singapore, Hong Kong, Thailand --."

"Oh MAN!" he interrupts. "You're hitting up all the good caves! Dank, soggy pussy just waiting for---"

********Do you see why I need alcohol? Do you see why it's social lube? Tranquilizer you shoot yourself with. In the face. Self-administered temporary lobotomy.**************

I don't remember when I fazed back in. Around the time my pint ran dry.

LeBron appeared to be off questioning other people.

"I need another drink," I announce.

"Yo get me one too, amigo! I'll pay you back. Not in BTC though aaaaayyyy! I'm keeping that shit on LOCK. This the HODL life!"

Back to the bar. Barman appeared busy. No, he noticed and walked over. A saint. True saint, that man.

Cold IPA this time. Name didn't matter. Neither did price.

I'd be a terrible drug addict.

No willpower.

The foam hit my beard. Second wind.

But before I dove back into battle, someone stopped me.
"Hold back a minute," said an old voice.
I turn to see the gentleman from the BTC meetup. Grey streaked hair. Salt and pepper beard trimmed close. Could have been a sailor marooned since WW2.
"Don't mind, Jack. The boy hasn't been laid in a while."
"No shit?" I say. "That charmer? That Bitcoin octopus? I hear girls around here go weak for tentacles."
He orders another water -- with ice. "Did I hear right? You're setting a leg in each county? One bitcoin to your name?"
"I am."
He considers this. "Then here's a piece of wisdom for your travels: You know what Bitcoin is?" He swirls his water. Ice hitting glass. "Bitcoin is freedom." He nods towards LeBron, off in the distance, prying answers from anyone who'll give them. "For some, Bitcoin is political freedom. A way to regain their human rights. An opportunity… for financial liberty." His gaze pulls me towards Jack. "For others," he pauses to let us bask in the glory that is Jack winning a belching contest no one called for. "For others, Bitcoin is a lambo to the moon."
"Yeah," I scoff. "And I'm sure soon as he got there he'd use his lambo to drive a dick into the moon --- big enough to be seen from earth."

The old man chuckles. "I would." He sips his water. "For all to see. My old shriveled dick. And grey hairy balls."

……

"God fuck." he continues. Why didn't BTC come around when I was your age." He chews through his ice. "One bitcoin." The ice grinds to nothing. "I'd give up my millions … for one bitcoin on a young liver and working cock." The waters gone.

"You're in for a wild trip." He turns to me, a grin to rival the Joker on his most manic day. Toothy, nicotine stained, wrinkled lips pulling back from old bones. "And you're not ready."

Then, I swear, he fucking fades away like the Cheshire cat.

DAY 17

Bullet train - China.
BTC remaining: 0.859 -- Net Worth: $4,617

Well now. That was creepy as shit. Three days later and it's still on my mind. Am I Alice? Was that BTC meetup a Mad Hatter tea party?

No. No, not yet. More like a glimpse. Foreshadowing. I'm still at the edge of the rabbit hole. I saw the white rabbit (bought a bitcoin), followed it (flew away from home), it plunged down the hole (the crypto world), but I'm still standing at the edge.

It's dark. Could be a long way down. No knowing what type of coked-out rabbits infest this pit and I don't have a Holy Hand Grenade.

LeBron took the leap. He spent the last few days digging deeper into Bitcoin. All our conversations revolved around it. He learned what all those buzzwords meant. He even started using them. Blockchain is decentralized -- no matter how much his government bans it, they can never shut it down. Seems he found his financial liberty.

He's meeting up with Jack -- to become a shrimp -- and buy his first bits of Bitcoin. After that they're going to party.

All I found was a splitting hangover and a vague sense of unease. Maybe I'm not ready to take the leap. Did you see the madness? The hype and "hopeium" Jack was snorting? Will that be me?

If I jump down this hole, go to those parties, surround myself with fake tits...will I end up strung out on hype, pushing BTC and dreaming of drawing dicks on the moon?

There's two kinds of people in this world. The ones who grab their balls and take that leap -- and those who chicken out and stay sane.

I seem to be a third kind of person: The guy who circles the rabbit hole, biting his nails, overthinking, and general unable to make a god damn decision.

This crypto world is leagues outside my comfort zone. Not only in terms of foreign lands, but also foreign ideas. Anarchy. Financial Liberty. No taxes.

Even the idea of fast money, getting rich quick -- is strange to me. Don't get me wrong. I'd love to be stupid rich. But up until now it's been a fantasy reserved for the rare $5 lottery ticket.

But Jack. He turned a few hundred dollars into 47 BTC currently worth north of $225,000. If that happens to me -- how will I change?

I don't know.

I should quit thinking. Make a decision. Take the leap or not.

Right now I'm enjoying the scenery. I'm currently racing away from Beijing at 280 km/h (a tick over 173 mp/h -- according to my rusty engineering degree). These bullet trains.

Damn. We're cutting through the landscape. If it weren't for the occasional tunnel I'd swear I was seated on a low-flying plane. Smooth, silent, fast. It's a beautiful thing.

Next stop: Pingyao. Jinzhong Prefecture. Shanxi Province. An ancient region of China. Rooted in the Han and Qin dynasties. The first humans to lay bricks in this city did so nearly 3,000 years ago. That's older than a handful of countries in Europe.

I doubt I'll find much in the way of Bitcoin or cryptocurrencies there. It's more of a pitstop, anyhow. My next big destination after this is the Chinese megacity Xi'an. 7 million people. The end of the fabled Silk Road. And the grave of the Terracotta Army.

Pingyao is on the way. Plus apparently it's worth seeing.

According to a few travel geeks on the internet, anyway.

DAY 18

Pingyao - China.

BTC remaining: 0.844 -- Net Worth: $4,681

Pingyao is worth it.

Holy shit. Yeah it's worth it. Pingyao is immersive ancient China. It's walking through a National Geographic cover.

Red round lanterns hang from curved tile roofs. Cobbled streets hold grooves from centuries of horse-drawn carts. Back alleys descend into crumbled walls. Rotting wood doors flaked in blue paint hang by their hinges. Rough grass sprouts from clogged gutters.

The air is pungent. Wood fires mix with crisp air flowing from distant mountains. Shallow puddles at street corners offer a satisfying splash for your boots.

The most fascinating moment, though, happens after you climb the steps to the top of the centuries-old stone walls guarding the town. Climb up. Take a few steps to the edge. Stop and look back.

There's the old town. Single story homes, occasional chicken coops, rutted alleys. You'd half expect an ancient order of ninja's to be headquartered down there; Bearded wise men and young apprentices, holding secret trainings on nights with no moon.

Then look outside the walls. Look beyond.

The modern city of Pingyao surrounds you. Streets swollen with traffic. Neon lights setting fire to dull concrete. And towers. Highrises. My god, look at all the highrises. Turn, turn, turn and all around you stand towers of glass and steel. The cold, efficient sentinels of industry.

No, you know what those tall, faceless towers look like?
Siege towers.
I swear, standing up there feels like being under attack. The old way of life behind me, guarded by several tons of brick and stone wall. The new way of life outside me, towers of glass, organized in full battle order, preparing to strike. A siege. Old vs. New.

Wood fires vs. electric heaters. Handcrafted baskets vs. mass-produced tote bags. Sweet & sour pork dumplings cooked from recipes passed down through generations vs. a Big Mac and coke.

When you're up on the wall, you're right in the middle. What a thought.

Either that or I watched too much Game of Thrones on the long train ride here. Yeah. That's it.

The heritage of this old town weighs heavy. You can feel it. A somber, serious place. No surprise, I suppose; since Pingyao is the birthplace of Chinese banking.

Since I'm attempting to travel the world on bitcoin -- this "magic internet money," these "junkie frequent flyer miles" -- I decided to stroll through the first bank to exist in China. Judging by its musty smell -- it could have been the first bank to exist on the whole Asian peninsula.

Picture it: A tall wooden facade. Imposing doors. Golden Chinese characters crowning the doors. They read: Rishengchang -- "Sunrise Prosperity." Adorning the heavy doors are long faded paintings of creatures: herons, dragons, lions -- guardians of the gold within.

Once upon a time -- in this country so far, far away -- only the most dignified and wealthiest of patrons would have been allowed in. Only the businessmen of the upper class would have been granted permission to stroll beneath those legendary guardians and through the grand doors.

Nowadays there's a rusty ticketbooth manned by a stumpy lady. She's got a single chin hair and she keeps stroking it like she ran out of fucks to give.

And now, through those majestic doors pour the great unwashed masses. Plebeians and tourists, every last man Jack of 'em.

The founding fathers of the first bank of China would roll in their graves, spin in their tombs, if anything of their bones was left to twirl.

Ironic. That's the word. The one word on my mind as I join the horde of lowborn day-laborers. Because, listen, what a change, eh? From a bank that was one of the most guarded places in all of China -- to a common tourist trap.

It blows my mind. Listen. This really stirs my brain sauce.

I toured the whole bank. What a place: The entry courtyard is designed with the most immaculate feng shui -- prosperity and wealth in every inch. Plush offices for bookkeepers and accountants, adorned in serious yet tasteful wood furniture. A reception room allowing the banks president to receive honored clients -- complete with an exquisite tea set which, I'm sure, accompanied an elaborate serving ceremony. Stables for the bank's very own security guard detachment. And the pièce de résistance -- a massive gold embossed gong -- in the shape of a gold coin; Once that gong served some sacred purpose. Now it's rung by any tourist with a dirty knuckle.

44

It gets better.

I joined the picture-hungry proletariat. We went on a tour of -- the vault. In the ancient days, to access this dragon's lair, you not only needed to know where the secret entrance was (a narrow staircase at the side of the building), you also needed to know the code -- and have a face the guard wouldn't punch. Then, once you were deep within the ancient basement you'd need to sign thick paper ledgers. The clerks down there, working only by candlelight flickering through oily smog, would take your deposit -- probably cackling like Gollum from Lord of the Rings.

But for us tourists the only difficulty is standing in a longass line. And when we finally arrive downstairs the air is clean and flooded by neon lights. Echoes of people saying "cheese" in fifty languages accompany camera pops. I can buy plastic souvenirs resembling fake gold bars. Battery operated monkeys drum out a beat. Why not buy a stack of fake 10,000 yen bills? They'll help your ancestors in the afterlife! If I don't watch my step I'll get gum on my shoe. The only security guard is a camera mounted in the far left corner -- and it looks like it ran out of battery in 1992.

This is what gets my brain stew boiling, right. Because just a tick over a hundred years ago this bank hummed in full operation. This vault would have been defended come hell or high water.

Now any philistine with two bucks can stroll in and carve a cock on the wall.

Let's put all this into context.

What if one day the big banks of the world, the banks you and I visit ... become tourist traps?

Imagine it. The bank you visit and trust. The vault holding your safety deposit box, with all your family jewelry, priceless mementoes, and unmentionable secrets. All that -- protected by heavy steel doors -- someday filled with casual tourists.

Let's take it a step further... to Fort Knox.

Fort Knox. The United States Gold Bullion Depository. 4,582 metric tons (147.3 million oz. troy) of gold. 2.3% of all the gold ever dug out of the ground. More than twice the gold held by the next leading country (Germany).

Fort Knox. Surrounded by electrified barbed wire, peppered with minefields, patrolled by unmarked Apache attack helicopters. 30,000 soldiers on 24/7 guard duty. Tanks. Actual, armed, tanks.

Fort Knox. So exclusive, so well and constantly guarded, it has been visited only once in the last 40 years -- and that was by Secretary of the Treasury Steven Mnuchin, not even a sitting president.

Now tell me, do you think that one day you will stroll into Fort Knox just as casually as I waltzed into this old bank?

If you said no. If you shook your head. If you snorted in disbelief and thought "nah" -- buddy, you haven't been paying attention.

The U.S. Government abandoned the gold standard nearly a hundred years ago (1933) and completely severed the link between the dollar and gold in 1971. What's all that gold doing in there?

If it's still there.

Mark my words, before too long, quite probably in our lifetime, you will be able to fly over to Kentucky, whip out your smartphone, and buy admission tickets for you and the family to good old Fort Knox.

The price? 0.00015 BTC.

And yes, you'll still be surrounded by armored tanks and attack helicopters -- but they'll be parked on the lawn. Kids will be crawling all over them like a goddamn jungle gym. And those 30,000 heavily armed soldiers patrolling 24/7?

More like 30,000 tourists armed heavy with juice bottles, jerky snacks, and holographic souvenirs.

DAY 20

Xi'an - China.
BTC remaining: 0.781 -- Net Worth: $4,533

I sold bitcoin to a Mongolian prostitute today.

Just putting that out there. Writing it down. A sentence I never thought I'd say. I sold 0.075 BTC -- to a sex worker -- who was Mongolian.

Yes, I jumped down the rabbit hole. If ever there was a moment to mark when, exactly, I took the leap after the little white rabbit --- this was it.

Why did I sell bits of my BTC? How did I manage it? What made me think she's Mongolian? And a streetwalker, no less? Stay seated. I'll tell you.

Yesterday. Middle of the night. 2am. The hostel silent as a grave. My bunk no bigger than a coffin and my mattress twice as hard. Laptop screen blazing across my face; eyeballs bloodshot, dry.

Rumblings on the web. Bitpay -- my VISA card provider -- isn't the most stable company. Access to my funds could be pulled from under my boots any time. If that happens ... 1/3 of my BTC is frozen -- waiting for a refund. And if it isn't refunded? If Bitpay gets hacked? My bitcoin stolen? Then I'll be the Mongolian whore.

Rather than run that risk (I don't have the cheekbones for it), I decide to get my hands on paper money. Convert a handful of my fairy dust for real cash.

Besides, I've already been turned away from several spots that only accept cash: hole-in-wall restaurants in Beijing, a cheap-as-dirt hostel in Pingyao, and most disappointing -- bars advertising cheap baijiu. That toxic swill. Red Dragon Piss. I'm missing out.

I need cash. But I hesitate. I've been hesitating for a while now.

Again, the only way to get cash is to sell my bits of bitcoin. For the uninitiated, there's a name for little bits of BTC; They're called "satoshi."

This honors the inventor of Bitcoin: Satoshi Nakamoto. By the way, I may not have mentioned this but ... no one knows who Satoshi Nakamoto really is. Could be an intelligent man. Could be a brilliant woman. Could be a group of elite white-hat hackers. Could be a well-funded government. Could be a room full of monkey's trying to type Shakespeare's masterworks but ending up with this formula for magic internet money.

No one knows. Wild.

0.00000001 bitcoin = 1 satoshi.

I decide I should sell 0.075 BTC (7,500,000 Satoshi). This amount should net me, at current prices -- 2,400 Chinese Yuan. That's $350 U.S. That should help me survive for the next two weeks.

I'm assuming the numbers are right. Accounting 101 was never my strong suit; The classroom had windows. Big picture windows; Looking out over the quad where all the good looking people went bouncing around. Just poor classroom placement over all.

0.075 BTC for cold hard cash. All I need to do is find someone willing to give me their hard earned money ... in exchange for electronic bits invented on the internet ... by a closet full of monkeys.

Stolen Wallets

Oh, and the President of China banned it. Oh right, and this magic soap bubble could pop any day now.

Fortunately, Xi'an is home to twelve million people. That's more than Los Angeles County. Statistics say I'm bound to find a nutcase or two.

So I get on localbitcoins.com and look for such a nutcase. My Satoshi for their Yuan.

What statistics didn't prepare me for is finding a dozen nutcases -- and needing to pick one.

That's why my eyeballs dried out after midnight. How to choose? How to choose someone who won't mug my ass. Someone who will make the transfer nice and easy and leave my liver where it is -- the comfortable spot between my lungs and stomach (also very vital organs that need to stay where they are).

I'm up late Binging reviews. God, that's weird to say. Bing-ing. Since Google is blocked by the 'Great Chinese Firewall' -- and I foolishly forgot to setup a VPN -- I resort to Bing. It's not half bad. Not sure what all the fuss is about preferring Google.

My Bing search terms are:

Is Localbitcoins.com a safe place to sell BTC? Localbitcoins safe yes no? Violent crime in China happen to tourists? How not to get stabbed in China. Legal sell bitcoin now china? Bitcoin selling public place safe? 14 signs you're about to get robbed. Hiding money in underwear smart? Hiding cash between buttcheeks good idea if clench real hard? Walking with money between asscheeks how to.

The search terms quickly descend into madness. Soon I'm reading horror stories of people getting drugged, waking up missing a kidney, needing stitches. Turns out that's all urban legend and myth. Doesn't stop me from trimming my fingernails with my teeth.

I need to sell my bitcoin for cash. No getting around it. But I need to be safe.

I settle on three verified, well reviewed local sellers, and email them. Close the laptop. Try to sleep. Wake up within minutes to the sound of notifications. All three are up and looking to sell. Who's up at four in the morning selling fiat for BTC? Sketch-ass people. That's who.

I set up a time to meet during daylight. 11am. Starbucks. Local Starbucks. That sounds good; they should have surveillance cameras -- which would be a great farewell gift for my family; condolences for their kidnapped son: grainy footage of his last moments drinking coffee before it was laced with daterape drugs.

It's 4am and I'm not in the cheeriest of mindsets. I try to sleep.

Within minutes a phone in the hostel room begins playing a wakeup alarm: cascading water slowly rising in volume. It's meant to be soothing. I want to step on it.

This is the price of hostels with rooms that sleep a dozen travelers. Someone's always getting in late, drunk and loud, waking everyone up. Someone else is always getting up early, still drunk, waking everyone up.

Earplugs are no use. The early bird hops out of his bunk below me. Begins packing. Shaking the whole bunk. He bumps into the lightswitch for the whole room. My closed eyelids offer zero protection against the light of a thousand suns. It burns.

He whispers "oh shit, sorry, sorry!" and flips the switch off. It's too late. He's become my sworn mortal enemy. If I ever win the lottery I'll find him. The night of his most comfortable sleep I'll shine a spotlight the size of Manhattan through his window.

Fuck it. It's over. No use sleeping. I'm suddenly hungry. Plus that waterfall alarm inspired my bladder. I climb down and go drain the main vein.

11am arrives fast. I'm sitting on a Starbucks couch. You know the kind. Coffee colored to hide the coffee stains. The place looks and smells like every Starbucks on the planet: pretentious.

Good coffee though. I can always rely on that. Or perhaps it's good because I spiked it with a few ounces of bijiu. My sleep deprived logic thinks the chemical alcohol will burn off any drugs. The back of my brain knows that's a lie. It's to bolster my courage.

A few minutes past the hour and the door opens. In walks my guy. The seller. Stick thin. Asian. Cropped jet black hair. My height. Basically an emaciated Jackie Chan. He's looking around; The way people do when they don't go to Starbucks for the coffee. We make eye contact. I wave. He nods. I stand up.

He walks straight past me. Goes to a table just behind me. Joins his friends.

I hate when that happens.

Grumbling, I unlock my phone to get clues on how the actual seller looks ....

"Hi!"

The brown couch rocks as a girl plops down right next to me.
"You are American buyer!"
"Uh, yeah." I protect my coffee from her peppiness. "How can you tell?"
"You look American! Very frightened. Very scared."
"No I'm not."
"Yes," she smiles happily, "you are!"
"And you are?"
"I'm Mongolian!" she answers proudly.
"No, I mean -- are you the seller?"

A bright "Yup" accompanies her head bob.
Color me surprised. I expected a dude. A crypto nerd or finance geek. Instead here's this Mongolian chic who appears to be the very definition of 'bright eyed and bushy tailed.' Big smile. Half-moon eyes above high cheekbones. Dark silk hair curling around an oval face the color of mocha. Quite exotic.
"You like?"
My brain stumbles back into gear. "What?"
She winks. Her hands playful twirl out to show off her curves, curves clothed in bright, almost eye-watering colors. The word 'flamboyant' comes to mind. Though I'm sure she would define it as 'fabulous.' Skin-tight orange pants. Frilly blue blouse. A big silver cross slipping between her tits.

> *Hold up. Just pause reading for a minute. Listen, time out. Big disclaimer right here, right now: I'm terrible at writing about me and meeting women. I'm the Steve Carell, Michael Scott from the Office, of writing about women, alright. I write the way I am in real life: awkward, bumbling, trying to act confident and failing miserably. Ask yourself, if 50 Shades of Grey was written by and starred Michael Cera -- would you read it? My stories aren't the polyamorous escapades of James Bond. I'm Zach Galifianakis trying to buy condoms at IKEA.*

> *So If you find yourself cringing too much -- skip ahead. You won't miss anything. Or put the book down. Throw it away. There won't be a quiz later. No Pulitzer Prize writing around here.*

****

"Yoouuu llliiikkke," she smiles. Again. Not a question.
I force my eyes back up. Damn bijiu in my coffee; it's loosening my

grip. I'm just trying to be a safe, non-muggable tourist. Is that too much to ask? "I need to sell my bitcoin."

"Ok!" She dives into her oversized purse, Coco Chanel (real or fake, I have no idea. Much like her tits). Whips out a cellphone. The case is a plastic smiling frog covered in sparkles. A few swipes later -- "Here! My deposit QR code."
I stare at her frog phone. "Right but, uh, do you...have the ...I'd like to see the ..... Money?"

She pouts. "Business, business. You no fuuuun." She pops open her purse again. Her hand dives in, nails painted in the colors of a Fruit Loops commercial. A bit of digging. Out pops a stack of Chinese Yuan. "Money!"
"Can I ... may I.... Count it?"
She playfully fans herself with the cash. "You have my BTC, baby?"
"Right, yeah." I fumble with my phone. Fuck up the unlock pattern. Twice. Open my Jaxx wallet. Show her my balance (rookie mistake. Stupid).
"Mmmm, baby boy American. You have more!"
"Haha, yeah. I'm traveling. 1 year around the world on 1 bitcoin."
"Ooooo! Big adventures!" She scoots in close. "You take me?" She purrs.
"Maybe the, uh, money bitcoin thing ... first?"
She gently smacks my nose with the cash. "You no fun." Then dangles the bills. "Send BTC."
"Can I... hold onto the cash?"
"Nooooooo," she says with a shake of her dark curls.
"Can I ... I don't know," trying to think fast all I can come up with is: "can we both hold each end of the cash?" #genius
"You think I run away?!" She turns up her little nose. "I'm not robber!"
"No no no no!" I backpedal. "It's, this is, well, it's my first time," and then quickly add: "selling BTC!"
This brightens her day. "First time for everyting!" She holds out the cash and winks. "Hold with me."

54

And there we sit …in a Starbucks stuck within the neon shopping center of Xi'an, China. Just a girl and a boy; her dressed like a Skittles packet and me like a lost American tourist; playing gentle tug-of-war with a stack of money. Surreal.

With a corner of the Chinese Yuan in my left hand -- I use my right to send the BTC to her: unlocking the phone, punching in 0.075, scanning her QR code, aaaannnddd send. "There. How many transactions do you want to wait for? Maybe 6? 30 minutes?"
She wiggles the cash we're holding and smiles. "This is romantic."
"6 is good right? yeah? 30 mins?" #uncomfortable
"You go to see Terracotta warriors? Very famous. Very close."
Too busy. Hadn't done the travel planning yet. "Not yet nope."
"You know…." she purrs. "I never go. Take me to see?"
"Oh, uh, maybe yeah." Why don't I just keep my mouth shut? 27 more minutes.
"Old history. Terracotta Army. Qin Shi Huang made army. He is first Emperor of China!"
"Oh yeah. Yeah I read that Xi'an is the start of the famous Silk Road."
She leans in to my face. "You want taste *my* silk road?"
"Uuuhhh"
"Good price." she tugs the cash in our hands. "Cash price."
"Uuuuuuuuhhhhhhh"
She leans in so close I catch her bubblegum breath, whispers "I like you -- frightened American …. for you special….. I no wear condom on my penis."
"Uuuuuuuuuuuuuuuhhhhhhhhhhhhhhhhhhhhh"

#longest25minsofmylife

DAY 22

Train leaving Xi'an - China.

BTC remaining: 0.778 -- Net Worth: $4,565

So that happened.

Lovely girl. Uh, guy. Um, person, human. Lovely. Just not my cup of tea right now. I mean, I just jumped down this rabbit hole. Give me some time. #SAIL

Transaction went smooth. I left with the money. She left with my Satoshi and a pouty face.

Didn't take her to see the Terracotta Warriors. My bad. She probably didn't want to see them anyhow, just see something else, if you know what I'm saying.

Right, well, I saw the Terracotta Warriors. A "Wonder of the World." Don't see what all the fuss is about. More like some zealous pottery teacher went on a bender.

Perhaps if I could have been close enough to see the warriors. Instead they're fenced off so far away I had to squint.

The crowds didn't help. Selfies flashing harder than a Hollywood red carpet premiere. Not sure if I was there to admire ancient archeological discovers or make duck lips at fake Insta followers.

Not much in the way of the fabled 'start of the silk road.'

A shame.

It once flung merchants to far corners of Asia in search of exotic goods. Emissaries embarked to play politics with foreign powers -- quickly followed by conquering armies. Now Xi'an is much like every other megacity: a sweaty mess of buildings being fucked by tentacles of highways like some neo-erotic Hentai porn festival.

There is a nice lake though.

DAY 40 SOMETHING??

Halloween Hangover -- Shanghai.

BTC remaining: 4,520 -- Net Worth: $0.735!

Wait.
Those numbers are wrong.

Eh, I'll fix it later.

Why my food hurt? Feet. My left and right foot. Oh. I'm missing my socks. The fuck happened last night. WHERES MY PHOEN??

frantic shuffling in bed searching every pocket, crevice, under pillow, everywhere God saw fit to make a space

"FUCKING QUIT IT!" *banging from the bunk below me*
Shit. I'm back at my hostel. How did I get here? I didn't walk, not with my foot like this … did I? I must have taken a cab. WHERE'S MY WALLET??
I scramble down the rickety ladder, shaking the whole bunk.
The curtains of the bunk below me fly open "DUDE! The fuck??"
"Sorry, sorry!"
"You JUST rolled in here an hour ago!"
(no wonder I'm disoriented as hell)
Other people in the room begin grumbling and shushing both of us.

Look at me. A few weeks ago in a hostel I was cursing a guy just like me. Now I'm the asshole.

I spot my pants on the floor. No wonder I could see the bandages on my leg. No pants. Grabbing them I feel the shape of my wallet and --. more important -- the shape of my phone.

Thank god. I'm not crawling back up that shaking ladder to my bunk. I've played the asshole enough. I rush out to the hallway, find the common bathroom, and stay put.

Phone first. Screen Isn't cracked. Turns on. Batteries near dead. Wallet? Still holds my cash and cards.

exhale

Holy shit.

I either have undeserved good luck or an equally undeserved guardian angel.

Now what the hell happened last night?

Lets see what my phone has to say. Before the battery dies.

Swipe it open. Photos. And ……. Oh. Wow…..

------Everything that happened last night (almost) -----

9p.m.

It's halloween. Like a loser -- I have no costume.

The hostel's about to host a Halloween pubcrawl. I am costume-less. Other hostel dwellers had the foresight to pick up a cheap mask, wig, or outrageous sunglasses. I chose to catch up on TV.

In my defence this hostel is the first place I've encountered real internet since flying into China. A convenience store around the corner had imported junk food. My bed became my cocoon. I only climb down to answer nature's calls.

Now I'm paying the price -- feeling like a loser.

People duck in and out of the room, costumed up and chattering with excitement.

I should get up and do something. This is why I'm here. This is why

Stolen Wallets

I'm traveling. Get out of my comfort zone. Not spend another Halloween ignoring the doorbell of life.
....
Eh, fuck em.
I do what a want.
Right now I want another bag of chips.
2 seconds later My phone vibrates.
It's that new messaging app: Telegram.
A message? From who?
Jack.
Jack from Beijing.
Jack -- HODL Lambo to draw a dick on the Moon -- Jack.
Hey bro. Where u at?
My fingers hover over the keys. Should I answer?
Nah.
But, well, he saw that I've read the message. Eh. Besides, Beijing is far away.
I text back: *Shanghai.*
Instant response: *brooooooooooooo* *sunglasses emoji, beer, bikini, 100, 100, 100* *that town is* *fire emoji* *hope you gettin cake!!!!* *wink wink wink*
Shit. What have I done? What to write back? *thumbs up* *Yeah it's nice.*
His texts come back fast: *??? its NICE ?? You're doing it wrong, shrimp.* *poop emoji* *look at my costume.*

He sends a pic. It's him in flip flops, sand colored denim shorts, pink Polo shirt, oversized sunglasses, and to seal the deal -- a fat red fanny pack. He's also pouring out a bottle of Hennessy. The caption reads: *I'm Rich Chigga, bitch!!! The pale ass Chinese Nigga!!*

Jesus. I mean, I guess asians can get away with it? I don't know.
He follows up with: *tell me you're packing your wiener for halloweener*
What? The hell is he on about? I write: *No I don't have a costume.*
His chat bubble pops up. Disappears. Pops up again. Disappears

60

again. This goes on for a furious five minutes. Then, clearly not finding the right words to express his outrage, Jack settles on the classic -- *FUCK YOU!!!!!* Quickly followed by: *put a fucking bag over your head and go! Go trick or eat some pussy!!!*

This guy. Real motivational speaker right here. Tony Robbins, Gary Vee, TED talk of inspiration.

I close the app and toss the phone away. Fuck that guy.

Problem is ... I happened to be watching Mythbusters on my phone.

I go to pick it back up.... but then it buzzes. My hand recoils.

It buzzes again. I leave it alone.

It stops buzzing. I get bored. Pick it up. Open it.

It buzzes five times in quick succession.

I ignore the messages. I resume my regularly scheduled programming. But the messages pile high: Threatening emojies. GIFs of middle fingers. Exclamation-point laced words. This guy missed his calling as a profanity spewing, party pushing life coach. I ignore them all.

But then he's calling me through Telegram.

I can't watch anything with my screen constantly flickering with a picture of his face. So I pick up.

"What?"

"Duuuuuuuude. SRSLY. Pack pack up your dick and GO."

"I don't have a costume."

"You're couchsurfing! Mooch off your host."

"No I'm in a hostel."

"Even better! Get your ass to the front desk. Ask for the lost & found. Free rummage sale. Boom. Done."

"I don't think --"

"Stop fucking THINKING! Grab some garb and go! Listen, there's this guy in Shanghai I know. A real crypto OG. A god damn whale. Bought bitcoin at a dolla. Can you imagine? A single dollar?? He's been ballin since 2012. His 'end of the world' party brought me to my knees!" I hear a pause, then with reverence often reserved for church he whispers: "his name ... is Pineapple Jesus."

"Riiiiiiight," I say, thinking hard about hanging up.

Jack steamrolls over my disbelief. "He's doing a Halloween party tonight. Gotta be. And you're going."
"No, man, I --"
"YOU'RE GOING!" shouts my unwanted life coach. "You're going and when you get there you'll say - you'll tell them - you'll say you were sent by me. But not my name! Not my real name. Pineapple Jesus baptized me a new name."
"No surprise."
"You NEED to know," he pauses so I have time to prepare for this passphrase, "you'll tell them you were sent by ...remember this ... you'll say you were sent by.... His Royal Highness Lord Cockblock -- Master of all Fuckups."
"what"
"Yeah he's a real asshole...... But in a good way! I mean it was my misstep. My fault. Epic party one night at his pad. He'd been hounding this ... this gorgeous woman all night, you know. I mean she was ... damn .. the sexiest .... Just sex appeal. She had it. And she knew it. And Jesus, he had her ready to pull him into the next room. They were flirtin. They were talkin.
And I ... well I mean they were flirting next to the food table ... who the fuck flirts next to the food table? Go to the ffff -- go to the bar!
So I walk over, high as fuck, so fucking high. And hungry... so hungry. I'd been giving them space. Been respectful.
But I'm hungry. And I go over there. I'm so hungry. Grab a fistful of baby carrots. And she's so gorgeous, right? She's just .... God damn... I want to wife her, okay. And I'm eating these carrots. They're so good. These baby carrots. Crisp, cold, wet. I'm popping these baby carrots like pills. I'm dipping them in hummus and sucking them off like dicks. Little carrot dicks. Hummus creamed carrot dicks.
Thinking about her. Just wanting her so bad, sooooo bad. But I know I can't have her. I can never have her. She's fuckin celebrity status, A-list, genetic perfection -- and I'm a ... I'm a fucking library card.

So now I'm angry and still hungry. So hangry. I'll never have her. She'd never even look at me. So I start biting these carrots, right. They're so crunchy. Satisfying crunchy. Chomping down on these baby carrots. Chewing through these carrot dicks.
Glaring at this woman, this perfect woman ----- and she …. She looks at me. And I mean, she's in complete disgust, every right to be. I've got hummus down my chin. Anger in my bloodshot eyes. Disgusting pig mess.
She glares at me……and I fucking melt. Melt like a Disney princess. Puddle on the floor.
She's an angel. Angel of death, sure - but an angel. I do the only thing I can think of….in my mindnumbing drunk love I … I need her to know my love for her …. Forever love … raise kids grow old love ….
I grab a, grab her olive, her martini olive out of her martini, and I get down on one knee, I bend the knee, and I grab her left hand. Just grab it. Take her hand.
And I….I slide the olive on her ring finger, slide that olive, hole first, on her ring finger …. And i ask her … I ask if … if she'll be mine. If she'll be my garlic princess. My garlic princess forever."
"……………………………………………………"
"……………………………………………"
"………………………………………"
"……………………………"
I crack a smile. "The fuck you did."
He busts out laughing. "Yeah I was suuuuuper high." He pauses. "Hey you're a good listener man. Thanks for listening. Ladies like that. Now go get some ladies! Go! I'll text him. I'll text Pineapple Jesus. I'll get you his postal code. You'll be in for a wild ass night. You'll love it. You'll call me and thank me. You'll call me on my cellphone. 'Hey. Hey Jack. Hey Rich Chigga. You the best. You're king. You're the whale's tail. I had a bomb ass time. I got cake by the ocean.' that's what you'll say. Right in my ear, through my phone, whisper it right in my ear. That's you."

God damn it. He's right. I'm doing this. The curiosity's already

Stolen Wallets

eating me alive. "Ok. I'll go."

"FUCK YEAH YOU WILL. Not a debate here, amigo. Not speech and debate. You're going! Just remember. Remember: you were sent express by ... bbyyyy?... bbbyyyyyy?"

Oh he wants me to answer. "I was sent by His Royal Highness Lord Cockblock -- Master of all Fuckups."
"That's right. That's right. CHAO!" *click*

Mythbusters relit my screen. I stared at it for a minute. My mind blank. The realization struck. Ah shit. What did I get myself into?

sigh no turning back. Time to shut up and lace up. Lock my stuff in my assigned cabinet. Visit the restroom. Wash my pits. Debate about really doing this. Force my lazy ass to commit. Go to the front desk.

The mousy girl behind the counter is absorbed in her phone. To be fair, there's no one in the hostel at this point. All partying. It's a ghost town. Poor girl's probably stuck at work.

Not wanting to startle her I say, gentle as can be, "Hey, sorry to bug."

She squeaks and drops her phone, eyes up and wide as anything. "Yes?"
"Sorry. Could I maybe rummage through your lost and found?"
"Wat?"
"Oh, haha. Well...So I forgot it was Halloween."
"Okie?"
"And I need a costume."
"Okai?"
"Can I uh, maybe, rummage through your lost and found?"
The little mouse processes this. She picks up her phone. Looks at it. Looks at me. "You want make costume?"
"Yup."

Processing… "From lost found?"
I smile hopefully. "Would be nice."
Processing…….
The little mouse lights up. "Fun!"
She uses all the might in her slim arms to tug a cardboard box from under the register. Then beckons me behind the counter. "Dress up time!"
I join her as she's burrowing in the box. "What do we have?"
A list of random items begin littering the floor around us, along with triumphant announcements for each one. "One sandal!" "Broken kitty umbrella!" "Empty water bottle -- with funny stickers! Battery banks! BIG plastic flashlight! Oooooo sunny's!" She models a comically large pair of Ray Bans. "Ripped jeans! Very fashion. OOOOO look: a BIIIIGG bra! For big boob American woman! Plastic flowers many colors!" She gathers them into a bouquet.
"A CD??" She flips the CD around with a confused look, staring at it. Metallica stares back at her. I zone out a moment as the CD takes me back to highschool for a minute. "And a big yellow hat!" She finishes announcing. She plops it on her tiny head.
The hat, a construction hardhat, sinks around her haircut. Cute. But…
I shake my head. "The hell am I supposed to do with all this?"
She thinks for a minute, reaches up and puts the hardhat on my head. Sticks the flashlight in my hand. Finds clear tape at the registry; tapes the CD -- shiny side up -- to my helmet. Then sticks plastic flowers in my beard and slings the bra around my chest. Finished and clapping, she happily introduces me to a small mirror. "See?! You are a transvestite!"
I laugh. "Very nice," then politely struggling to take off the bra, I say. "But I'm not that brave."
pouty face
"No hey, you gave me an idea."
"YMCA man?"
"No, a miner."
"Huh?"

"Do you have some cardboard I could cut out?"
"Maybe."
"And some yellow sticky notes."
Working fast, I cut a big B out of the cardboard. Then tape sticky notes on it. It now resembles the Bitcoin B symbol. Perfect. Then a shoelace from a single lost sneaker -- and -- bam! Hung around my neck shines the Bitcoin symbol.
"There!"
She squints. "What you are?"
I tap by hardhat and rattle my bigass flashlight. "I'm a Bitcoin miner!"
"Oh."
"Clever right?"
She wrinkles her nose. "You look like trash."
I shrug. "Yeah, well, I am trash, so..."
Her shrug flops under the weight of her disappointment. "Whatever."
Yeah. Hm. Maybe a bit of flare? I eye the sparkly bra with its cups large enough to baptize children. No. No I'm not that brave. Not yet. I know it's why I'm on this journey; to challenge myself. Get out of my shell. Live a little. But I'm not there yet. Call me lame. I can't do it.

I thank her and exit stage left. The party is forty minutes walk away. I'll hoof it. See the town.

It's a Tuesday. Nearly midnight. Cold October snap forcing my hands in my pockets. Makes no difference to these locals. Life surrounds me.

Neon lights blaze above humid karaoke bars where windows rattle to K-pop mixed with 90's Americana. Ramen restaurants spill their sizzling sounds, aromas, and lines of hungry customers onto the streets. People jostle their way around like water swirling around eddies. All rather ... generic. Until I cross into the posh district.

Like crossing a line. An invisible line. Unspoken, unmarked, yet very much real. From the normal hustle and bustle of blue-collar people scrubbing out a living -- to opulence, extravagance, excess.

You see it in the cars. Korean Kia's give road to German BMW's. You see it on the streets. Outdoor noodle bars packed with friends sharing a laugh come to an end --- indoor hibachi grills begin ... attended by people who've lost conversation topics and need the distraction of an underpaid chef to flip bits of flaming shrimp in the air.

You see it in apartment windows. Back there I'd catch glimpses of families still awake, chatting and cleaning up after dinner together. Now all I pass are IKEA catalogues, the only sign of life a beautiful purebred dog, well groomed and fed -- staring out the window -- lonely as fuck -- looking as if he hasn't ever been scritched behind the ears. Not a pet; a god-damn showpiece.

You know what this city feels like? Feels like old money. Dirty old money.

The buildings beside me stand immaculate. British colonial mansions. Apartments and offices from Art Deco times. Imperialism. They sit low and elegant, dimly lit in their opulence. The horizon above them bright as anything. Pierced by skyscrapers made out of glass and big fat stock options. Dirty old money washed clean. Watch it shine.

Maybe I'm biased. I walk these extravagant streets and remember that time my buddies and I were sharing a pie at Old Town Pizza, back home in Portland.

He pointed out what looked like a trap door on the floor. Then he said it was, in fact, real. A "deadfall" trap door. Said there were dozens all across Portland. In old saloons, pubs, whore houses. All connected through a maze of tunnels. The Shanghai tunnels, as they were called. Why?

Well, used to be that loggers, cowboys, sheepherders, regular working stiffs, would go out for a pint and a game of cards, shoot some pool, -- and get taken. Grabbed off the streets, slipped knockout drops in drinks, or dropped through deadfalls.

Imagine that. Going for a beer after work, then taking a piss, and in the middle of shaking out the last drops -- suddenly falling through the floor -- and getting your lights knocked out.

These gents would then wake up either in cells below ground, waiting until they'd be forced onto ships -- or already on the ships. Ships leaving for -- Shanghai.

That's where the term "Shanghaiing" came from. Surprise, surprise.

Forced labor from Portland, Seattle, San Francisco -- all bound for Shanghai. Taken and forced to work their way back home. Forced to sail on old-ass ships, for at least two full voyages --- that's six years --- just to get back to Portland. To get back home.

Portland used to be the most dangerous port in the U.S. because of this. The "Shanghai capital of the world."

Now I'm here. In Shanghai. Of my own free will.

No one drugged me. No one knocked me out. Maybe that'll change soon....

Before I know it, I'm standing in front of the mid-rise apartment building marked on my GPS. The address Jack gave me -- that Rich Chigga.

What a place; Industrial concrete covered in mirrored glass and "pre-rusted iron." The entry doors could fit an elephant. The lobby within showcases a gold-flecked marble floor, obsidian black walls, and minimalistic seats designed to discourage sitting. A pretentious pile of architectural vomit, is what it is.

Am I ready to meet Pineapple Jesus? Tell him who I was sent by? Party with crypto bros?

Who knows. Perhaps I'll get reverse-Shanghaied. End up on a containership bound for Portland. Wouldn't that be a trip?

Alright. Alright. Time to adjust all this trash I've decorated myself with, sack up, and ring the bell.

Let's see. Apartment #(redacted for privacy).
beep beep *beep beep*
Nothing.
Did I ring the wrong one?
Apartment number (redacted)
beep beep *beep beep*
Nothing.
Shit.
Uh. Shit. Now I'm standing out on a street lined with cars worth more than both my kidneys. I'm dressed in garbage. At least I won't get mugged.
One more ring.
beep be---
*Click. *Sounds of insane partying in background**
"BLESS YOU, MY CHILD!"
A car alarm goes off.
"Uhhh. Amen?"
"Recite the Lord's Prayer and enter!"
What? What kind of 'Eyes Wide Shut' shit is this? "I was told to see Pineapple Jesus."
"Myriad faithful flock here to touch the frock of our savior! Look at the camera and recite the crypto vows!"
"Uuuhhhhh," I squint around me. "Where the hell is the camera?"
A floodlight blazes above the keypad.

Surprised laughter "Oh no. Oh you poor lost soul. What is it you're wearing? Oh no." The light gets brighter. "Did you go dumpster diving outside an office supply store, my boy?" chuckles the com. "What's that B on your chest?"

"Bitcoin."

More merry laughter "Cut it out of a pizza box, my son? Sacrifice the main wall of your homeless shelter to make it?"

"I'm a Bitcoin miner."

"Shitcoin miner, more like," continue the chuckles. "Who, pray tell, would send such a lost and cheapass sheep to a divine party such as this?"

I squint through the light. "His Royal Highness Lord Cockblock -- Master of all Fuckups."

A pause. A long pause. "Son of a bitch."

more partying

A heavy sigh "Bless that little chigger, for he knows not how much he pisses me off."

The door buzzes.

"Enter, confused and penniless boy -- and see the light."

"Uh, which flo--"

"The penthouse suite -- naturally."

click

Through the posh lobby, into one of the half dozen posh elevators, and all the way to the posh top.

The penthouse door is rattling from the music. It's rattling on its hinges. Those must be industrial strength hinges. Party loud enough to make me wonder if Pineapple Jesus bought the apartment below this one too -- just to cut down on noise complaints.

I ring the bell. Nothing. Knock. Nothing. Pound on it.

Door opens.

I'm fucking blinded by the light. As if St. Peter's blessed Pearly Gates opened forth before me. Except instead of heavenly angels on melodious harps -- it's a wave of bass heavy EDM. And instead of white-bearded Saint Peter in a toga and roman sandals -- it's a black guy in a suit and tie like Jules Winnfield from Pulp Fiction. Do I look like a bitch?

Decked out in all this secondhand garbage -- yes I do.

He steps forth, every inch the perfect replica of Samuel L. Jackson. A gold chain rests round his neck with a gold pineapple hanging heavy, gleaming. "So you're the shrimp."
"I'm the shrimp."
He lowers his shades. Examines my trash-stume. "What an incredibly sad and pathetic attempt."
I laugh, "story of my life."
"Amen to that sorry, sorry truth." He slides his shades back on, blazes a smile, and throws his arms wide. "Nevertheless! Pineapple Jesus welcomes all the lost and lonely sheep!" Then holds up his golden namesake. "Kiss the holy pineapple -- and be welcomed into the kingdom of heaven!"
I stare at the sacred fruit, big as a fist. Did everyone kiss it? Disgusting. But the party far down the hall is raging. Music, laughter, drinks. Is that a girl riding a mechanical bull?
Eh. Fuck it. What's the worst that could happen.
I lean over and peck the medallion. Tastes like strawberry lip gloss.
He claps my shoulders. "WELCOME!" Then -- being taller than me -- wraps an arm around my shoulders and leads me inside. "Jack tells me you're stepping 'round the world using only one bitcoin?"
"Yeah I'm trying."
"Adventurous little shrimp. Like finding fucking Nemo." He raises an eyebrow. "What's your Nemo?"
I can't answer right away. My brain overloaded by the sensory mindfuckery around me. The hallway we're walking through is wider than a bowling lane. It's lined with art. Custom art.
I just walked by a painting of him on the cross. A black guy on the cross. With a gold chain hanging Bitcoin around his neck. I'm not religious -- but that's a mind bender right there.
"My Nemo?"
"Your Nemo. Your purpose. Your goal."

"Uhhhh. I don't know."
"Mmmmmm. Truly a lost and lonely little shrimp."
We exit the hallway. I stop dead. Shocked.
"Welcome!" He exclaims with a sweeping hand. "To the crypto cathedral!"
This cannot be real. How does this exist? How does this place, is this, how in the, am I looking at reality right now? People say 'truth is stranger than fiction' -- but no one will believe me. I'll write this down later -- in my log journal (like I'm doing right now, hello there), and no reader/viewer/podcast listener -- will believe me. It's -- holy brick shitting shit -- how do some people have this much goddamn money? To burn? In this way?

The domed ceiling shows a fresco of Michelangelo's 'The Creation of Adam.' The one with God and Adam almost touching fingers. Except it's God giving a golden pineapple to Samual L. Jackson. This inspiring work of art drips down the Romanesque columns to a floor of simple grey concrete -- splattered in wild colors.

Everything seems to be bitcoin themed. There's a gigantic Bitcoin 'B' tiled in gold at the center of the massive circular parlor. Parodies of famous art line the walls: the Napoleon-on-a-horse painting but instead -- depicting a cartoon bitcoin riding a horse and conquering armies of paper money; Andy Warhol's soup but with bitcoin; Banksy's riot guy throwing flowers -- except he's throwing, yes, a goddamn bitcoin.

Then, next to the bar, there's a Statue of David but instead of a fig leaf covering his manhood -- it's a bitcoin. Beyond all this are floor-to-ceiling windows overlooking the Shanghai skyline -- dazzling at this time of night.
Inside, the Halloween decorations are without equal. Crimson curtains drape over plush couches. Silver wrought candelabras hold candles flickering with live flame (he must have emptied every smoke detector of its battery). And the people. The guests. My 'Bitcoin miner' costume is a hopeless embarrassment.

There's a DJ wearing a marshmallow helmet with X's for eyes that pulse to the rhythm. His music washes over a crowd dressed to the nines: everything from the traditional 'gothic vampire' to Charlie's Angels.
But then there's Kim Jung Un -- break dancing. And a woman who somehow made a bottle of Sriracha look sexy. There's a guy dressed up as Weird Al grinding on another guy dressed as a bare chested Terminator. A topless Pikachu making out with Harry Potter. Doctor Who and that one girl from Firefly. Everywhere I look it's a reddit board dedicated to terrible, horrible, no-good erotic fanfic.

"Come," beckons the host, "I'll introduce you."
We circle the dance floor, heading to the bar. Even from this distance I see the glass shelves glittering with every famous bottle of Hard-A known to man. It's not a watering hole so much as an oasis. And the revelers around it are thirsty.
We stroll up to the Asian versions of Captain America, the Joker, and a massively bearded character I don't recognize. They raise their martini glasses as a salute. "Evening, PJ."
Our gracious host waves his hand. "Gentlemen," he claps my back. "A new shrimp in our pond."
I extend a polite hand. "Hey, hi, hey," it goes as we shake hands.
"He's embarked on a journey. Around the world on one bitcoin."
Murmurs of appreciation.
"I leave him in your care. Get him a Moonshot and a Bitcoin On The Rocks. Show him how whales party."
Captain America turns to the bartender and speaks a few lines of manderin. The strange new drinks begin the first step towards my liver. Meanwhile, the Joker says: "So, one bitcoin huh?"
I nod.
He turns to the barbarian guy. "I've never had one bitcoin."
The barbarian, with a voice hidden by his fake beard, replies: "Least I've had was 58. Mt. Gox took the rest."
"Fuck Mt. Gox. I would have been a billionaire by now."
"Fuck Mt. Gox." They toast to this.

Captain America turns back to us and hands me a shot glass and an old fashioned tumbler. Both near overflowing. The shot is clear with a drop of red dissipating in it. The tumbler is electric green -- the color in a liquid cooled gaming rig --- and it's steaming.
"Moonshot first," he says, pointing to the shot glass.
I try and think of a clever toast. "To Satoshi Nakamoto. Long may he remain anonymous."
They approve, lifting their martini's. "Long may he remain anonymous."
Down the hatch. Whoa! Woo. hot. Damn that's hot. (Moonshot = hot sake with a drop of something spicy.)
Now a taste of Bitcoin On The Rocks. Oh damn. A snap of cold. Fuck that's refreshing. Can't quite place it though. "What's in it?"
Joker smiles. "Liquid nitrogen cooled sake and gin tumbled over green tea liqueur cubes."
Damn. That's intense. "No beer around here, huh?"
"Not a single drop."
Fancy fucks. Though I must admit: this drink packs a punch. And what's this? What's this at the bottom of the tumbler? "Is that .. is that a bitcoin?"
"Souvenir coin. Nice touch eh?"
At the bottom, distorted by ice cubes and alcohol, rests a coin big as a silver dollar -- but gold -- and stamped with the Bitcoin B. A nice touch indeed.
"That was PJ's idea," says the captain. "How do you know him by the way?"
"Oh, first time meeting him," I continue refreshing my liver. "You guys know Jack? From Beijing?"
A round of head shaking.
"Lord cockblock? Master of all fuckups?"
That gets a round of laughs.
"What a jackass," Joker chuckles.
"But a good jackass," the barbarian points out.
They nod.
"Hey," I ask the bearded barbarian looking chap, "Who are you supposed to be anyway?"

"Zhang Fei."
I reply with a blank look.
"Famed military general."
"Ah."
"You have the beard for it," he points to the birdnest on my jaw.
"But instead you're dressed as a….?"
I hesitate, rather embarrassed. "A Bitcoin miner."
"Not gonna lie," remarks Captain America. "You look like an oversized fleshlight -- carrying a smaller, normal sized fleshlight."
They laugh. I join them. Not a bad roast. "Yeah, well. Last minute. Stuff from a lost and found."
"PJ's got a heart of gold, eh?" Says the captain to the Joker. "Letting the shrimp in."
"Heart of Bitcoin," the joker corrects.
"How do you guys know him?"
"From the parties. Always puts on a hell of a party."
Murmurs of agreement.
"Well…how'd he get called… you know? Pineapple Jesus?"
"Simple," explains the barbarian. "Provides loaves and fishes," he points to the food bar, stacked with what appears to be cake and caviar. "Turns water into wine," thumbs at the bar -- where there's a fountain which, through clever illusion, seems to be turning water into wine. "Rescues the poor," he points to me. "And he makes his bitcoins multiply."
Captain America adds, "I heard it was because he eats pineapples everyday -- the ladies love it."
My eyebrow bounces off my hairline. "What? Why would the ladies --"
"Turns his cum into candy."
My other eyebrow joins the first one up there.
The Joker laughs at the captain. "How you know that? You tried it?"
"Heard from my side chick."
"She get in his pants?"
"Yeah."
The barbarian laughs. "You enjoy PJ's leftovers?"

Captain A shrugs. "Trickle down economics."

They laugh.

These crazy rich asians. They're Americanized accents and lingo throws me for a loop. "So how'd you guys get rich?"

Joker pipes up. "Stupidest way possible," he laughs. "I bought dogecoin."

"The joke coin? Doesn't it have a dog on it?"

"Yeah," he laughs. "It went up. So I used the profit to scoop up all the dumbest bullshit out there." He raises a hand and begins counting off fingers. "Pizzacoin, sexcoin, analcoin, fuckcoin, Spankchain, asspace ... uh...just ... all the bullshit ... was there a bullshitcoin? I don't know. Probably picked that up too."

"And you just ... made money?"

"Sure. It's all about timing. Timing and finding a coin with good marketing. Everything else is worthless."

The barbarian butts in. "You got that backwards. Bitcoin's the only true coin. Everything else is worthless."

Joker scoffs. "Listen to the bitcoin maximalist over here."

"It's fucking true though," he barrels on. "This is our generations gold rush. Gold rush of the fucking century. The first digital asset. Digital gold. Trustless, immutable, decentralized. Deflationary, not to mention. U.S., E.U. -- our China -- they're all printing money. All inflating the shit out of our money. Making it worthless. Boiling us alive, slowly, but yeah.

And, and, with Bitcoin it's deflationary. The only one. Fixed supply. Halving every four years. And what about all the bitcoins lost every year, huh? The Bitcoin's I've lost. You've lost dozens. Forgetting your private keys last year."

"Yeah that was a shit day. Shit month. Shit year!"

"So there goes the supply shrinking. Like gold bars lost at sea. Sunk. Gone. Supply goes down. Price goes up. HODL on."

"And if people stop buying btc, hm?" argues the Joker. "So what if you have the rarest Beanie Baby ever made. If no one wants it -- no one wants it!" He downs his drink. "It's all happening to us in the end. Buy the idiocy. Sell the marketing."

"Short-sighted as shit," rolls the captain. "Bitcoin, blockchain,

they're allowing capitalism to move onto the internet. Look at Ethereum. Look at cryptokitties."
"Aw for fucks sake," says the bearded barbarian.
"No look. Look at it. You can own a cryptokitty."
"I bought a hundred," says the Joker with a pleased smile. "Stupid as shit. Great marketing. Love em."
"Yeah. You own them. Digital ones and zeros. No pirate can take them. They're yours."

I'm confused and need to clarify. "Is that part of the goldrush? Cryptokitties?"
"Fuck yeah," shouts the captain. "The goldrush is owning digital bytes and kilobytes. "Most of it's fools gold. But there are nuggets in there."
The barbarian looks disgusted. "That is the single cheesiest metaphor you've said. Nuggets of gold. What's wrong with you, man? You're drinking a martini -- not a fucking Capri-sun -- act like it."
"All I'm saying is that Bitcoin is a revolution. It's the revolution, man. The REVOLUTION."

"Uh." I but in again. "Why? Why's it a revolution?"

The barbarian turns to me. "Listen, shrimp. I'm no Pineapple Jesus. I don't do questions. You want to know what Bitcoin really is?" He turns to the bartender. "Hey! Get this guy another drink!" Back to me. "Get your ass in the crowd. Check out PJ's pad. Talk to people. Then you'll see what BTC's all about. You'll see what it's worth. What it does."
"Hey," says Joker, getting out his phone. "What's your telegram? I know some people you might find ... uh ... fascinating."
He finds my handle, I thank him, and -- drink in hand -- I leave the three douch-cateers to their arguing.

Time for some ground level reporting. Not that my reporting would be worth anything -- my rising blood alcohol level would prevent that. Plus my costume is intimidated by all the better costumes.

So I wander. I walk. Take a self-guided tour of the penthouse. Just walk -- like the loser kid at a party, wandering around so people think he has a purpose, a place to be. Better not get in that guys way. He has places to be. Important places. Whoa. Wish I was him. Wish I was that guy. He's, he has places. Places to be. Wow. Man. Everyone's full of envy. Envy me. I have places that need being ... in....In those places. That's where I need to be. That's where I'm going. To those places. Where I need to be. ASAP. Watch me now. Watch me go to them. Wish you were me. But you're not. Haha. Fuck you.

This place is huge. I still haven't been in the same room twice. I didn't go for a tour. This place is Australia and I want on a damn walkabout. Aborigini walkabout.

It has two more full bars. One on the outside terrace and one in the master bathroom, of all places. I refilled me beverage. Both times. Twice each.
And I saw things. I drank and I saw things.

Here's a play by play, right.

The balcony gets my feet first. I go there. To the windows overlooking a city of 30 million people. And it isn't a balcony. It isn't one of those balconies you stand on for a smoke. This is an outdoor terrace. A garden on top of the world.
Panorama's in all directions overlooking a neon night so bright you can't see the stars. The wind carries the cold of October and the sound of highways; mixes with all the weed being smoked up here. Two dozen revelers slowly getting stoned.
Marie-antoinette in French frills puffing a blunt fat as a Cuban cigar -- passing it to the Genie from Aladdin, who coughs as if it's his first time; puff pass to Indiana Jones -- who's laughing at the Genie.

Off in the corner James Bond is making out with a "sexy" bowl of popcorn. Next to me there's the entire male case from Dragon-Ball-Z discussing, in depth, if KFC in China is better than the KFC in America. Soon enough they launch on a quest to go get a bucket -- and then apparently catch the first flight to L.A. for a fresh side-by-side comparison.

Hungry now I follow my nose to the kitchen.
Bowls of fresh fruit are going ignored in favor of various piles overflowing with candy. Just dumped on the counters. Gummy bears falling on the floor and leaving squished messes; half eaten Twix bars; full sized Snickers; empty pizza boxes full of Skittles; sour patch kids but it looked like someone licked the sour off a few and then put them back. All scattered around drink cups stacked together like the skyline outside. A cornucopia of sugar. My teen self would have loved it. Especially the three girls each dressed like Sailor Moon -- with their blonde wigs off and their faces stuffed with Almond Joy's. But they were surrounded by three times as many dudes in various Avatar, Batman, and Samurai (or some shit) costumes -- each one macking on them. So I leave.
There's a theater room, because of course there is. No one's watching Kill Bill. They're all having various kinds of sex. So I leave that well enough alone.
Then there's the master bedroom with its bar in the master bathroom. The opposite of sex is going on in there. It's a convention of intellectuals.
They're sitting on couches, edges of the bed, and leaning against walls. They're discussing using cryptocurrencies to overthrow the banking system. How Bitcoin can help them run for President of Taiwan. Fast ways to funnel millions of Yen through Macau casinos using Litecoin. Where they can buy a Lambo at this time of night -- for Ethereum. And more such incredibly ambitious plans. I soon find the reason for such spurred intellectual debate: with every drink at the bathroom bar you get a small mirror with a complementary line of coke.

5 star service right there. Hilton can go fuck itself.

Then there's the office with a few costumed guys hunched over their laptops. I ask and one says they're "trading shitcoins so we don't miss the pumps."
The bedrooms have more sex going on.
The library has a big screen showing a basketball game. People are shouting at it and placing bets -- using their phones.
The bathrooms, spacious and nice, have lines in front of them. Must be universal no matter how big the house.
So I drag my feet back to the crypto cathedral. Admire the artwork for awhile. Then feel lame and decide to prowl the edge of the dance floor.

It's a wild mess. Some guy who's both beauty AND the beast (going for clever points?) is stumbling around high fiving all the girls. Bunch of people who look like they're on Molly keep dancing as if they're glued together.
There's a girl in an inflated pumpkin costume laughing hysterically as her friend in an inflated sumo costume tries to grind on her.
The stoners have wandered inside and are asking the DJ where the snackbar is.
A few coked out guys are attempting to network by handing out business cards. It's a royal shitshow -- and it's beautiful.
I'm about to dive in when I catch sight of the best costume yet: A girl/woman dressed up as Albert Einstein. And not "sexy Albert Einstein" either (whatever that might look like). No. Full on wild white hair, lab coat, coffee-stained pants.
She's leaning against a column, as amused by the display of craziness as I am.
For a moment I forget my shitty costume and, acting on a drunken impulse, walk over.
"Hey, uh, E=MC2, huh?" <--- actual line. Great job, brain. Real clever.
She turns her eyes up at me and smiles quizzically, "What?"

"Uh," I stumble. "You're costume. Albert Einstein right?"

"Oh, no," she laughs. "I'm Satoshi Nakamoto."

Well color me dumb as bricks. I laugh it off. "Wow, yeah okay. haha. Cool." <--- again. actual line. fuck my neadrethal brain, am I right?

She gives my costume an updown. Smiles. Genuine too. Not like all the sarcastic smiles and mocking thumbs-up I've been getting all night. "You're a bitcoin miner, huh?"

"Yeah, haha." <--- by the way, I'm very literally saying 'haha' That's how nervous I am.

"Cool."

Ages of silence. Decades. Centuries.

"So how do you know Pineapple Jesus?" Hand to god, the only question I could think of.

"We used to go to grade school together."

"Really?!"

"No," she laughs, not looking my way.

"Oh."

"So….first time?"

Her smile's thinner this time, but no less bemused. "You should be dressed up as a detective. Get your interrogation spotlight and all."

"Sorry, haha." Fucking stop saying that already.

Ages slide by again.

"My first ti--" I say as she says

"Well I'm getting a dri--"

"Right, yeah! Go for it!"

Another bemused look. She turns to go. I pretend to nonchalantly watch the dance floor as if I'm thinking of getting out there. You know. Smooth. Lean against the column. Slip a little. Recover.

"Hey, you thirsty?" she calls back.

"Uh, yeah! Always. Alright. Yeah."

Back to the bar. Back to where this night started. Though the three musketeers aren't around.

"Have you tried the, uh, Bitcoin on the rocks?" I say, attempting at the knowing of cool things.

Stolen Wallets

"Not my thing."
"Oh, yeah. Weird steam and shit."
She orders a beer.
"I thought .... They didn't have beer?"
"PJ?" she asks, skeptical. "He's got everything."
"Oh. It's my fi--"
"First time, yeah, got it."
"Haha." shoot me.
She takes a swig. "So why is it your first time here?"
"I'm traveling," I say with a headbob. Then order a beer. "Around the world on one bitcoin."
That seems to snag her attention. "One bitcoin, huh?"
"Yup."
"Why?"
shrug "Learn about bitcoin. Travel a little. Never traveled before. See the world."
She laughs and shakes her head.
"What?"
"You have no idea why you're doing this huh?"
I shrug. Take a swig.
"You know," she offers, "if you're really after bitcoin ... you're in the wrong place."
I raise an eyebrow. "How so?"
Her eyes direct mine to look over the dance floor, the crypto cathedral, the terrace, the whole party. "The real innovators, the real thinkers -- they're not at this party," she says. "They're never at these parties."
"Are there better parties?"
Her eyes settle on the glowing skyline of this sleepless city. "They're out there -- working away. Working right now. For them, their work, improving the blockchain, tweaking the hashrate, it's better than snorting all the blow at this party." She sweeps her glass across everyone here. "Bitcoin isn't people partying. It isn't the people out on the balcony talking big. It isn't the people in the office trading....It's the people you don't see. At home. Glued to their monitor. Reading whitepapers, coding, and rubbing one

out," she says, complementing it with the typical hand jerk motion. "Those are the people changing the world."
Silence as I take this in.
"So what are you doing here?" I say, then backtrack immediately. "Not that you're not one of those, uh, real thinkers/innovators, or something."
That small, bemused smile is back. She seems to consider answering. "I'm a camgirl."
"................................oh" That statement hit me like a truck.
"I show my pussy for Bitcoin."
And that one backed the truck right back over me.
I can't think of anything to say. Say something! I need to say something. Anything! Break the silence. Complement her. Tell her she's brave. No that's pandering. Be chill about it. Say that's awesome; She's an entrepreneur. No that's stupid. Tell her she's cool. No that's lame. Ask where I can see her perform? No that's creepy. Creepy as fuuuuuuck. No. Uh. Get her another drink. No that's diverting the subject; Grow a pair! Think of something suave and sophisticated goddammit!
"So, uh, how much does it cost? Do I pay? Like, people pay?"
what in the almighty FUCK?! Creepyassdumbass brain…..i swear to everloving…brain…I will pull you out that skull and beat you with jumper cables. "I'm sorry, I didn't mean, haha, no I --"
"It's okay." She's enjoying my death-by-embarrassment. "You have a whole world to see. My show would break your piggy bank in a week." wink.
"Oh yeah? Haha." I rub the back of my neck, as one does in these awkward moments. "Yeah I just started. Can you tell? You can tell huh?"
"Mm-hm." She nods. "One small shrimp in a big, big pond." She finishes her beer. "See you around."
With a smile, she leaves. There she goes. Cutting through the heaving mass of people -- most of them halfway out of their costumes by now.
Her wild white hair fades from view as the music fades back in,

bass heavy and pounding.

I lift a few more drinks. Try to dance. Explain my costume fifty more times. Wander around. Share a joint with a school of ninjas. Stand at the edge of the terrace/balcony/building for a bit. Notice the little souvenir bitcoin in my pocket. Flip it around my fingers. Think about what she said -- about all the real innovators out there. About all the party rockers in here. And where I fit in. If I fit in.
Then I walk home.
Get lost. End up walking for 2 hours. Trash my socks.
Find the hostel. Somehow by the grace of god.
Climb up my bunk -- hear complaints from fellow hostel bunkmates.
Pass out.

TO BE CONTINUED

\-\-\-\-\-\-\-\-

"What?" I hear you say. Followed quickly by "What the fuck?!" and then "Is this guy serious? That's it? I paid for half a book?! What an asshole!"

It's true. Both of those things are true. You paid for half a book. And I'm an asshole for only publishing half a book. I'm sorry for letting you down a bit here, loyal reader who made it to the end of the first half.

I'll make it up to you. But first let me wordvomit a few excuses.

1) I'm not the best writer. My teachers always said my handwriting looked like chicken scratch -- I suppose they were too kind to tell me it read like chicken shit. This book seems fit for maybe five people on the planet. If you enjoyed it -- you're one of them -- and I wish we could sit down for a beer, you strange person, you.
2) I don't have a fat wallet. Nor do I have a lucky penny tucked away in my sock drawer. After my journey I spent my remaining savings on hospital bills and recovering from various illnesses I gathered in Cambodia, India, and Egypt. I wrote this first half of the book while recovering.

Now that I have a job, I've tried to write while working -- but one job just isn't enough. I'll need to look for a side hustle. So, when this book begins to sell well -- and enough $ is flowing in for me to work just one job instead of 1.5 -- then I'll start wrapping up the rest.

Speaking of the rest, here's a cornucopia of crazy shit I'll write about in the second half:

1) A guy living in Shenzhen who scammed his Kickstarter backers out of over $100,000. He promised to create a VR device that shows porn -- and sucks your willie in-sync to what's happening in the porn. Naturally hundreds of guys pledged their money. Only to have this guy take it all to China -- and stay there. This guy. What a piece of work. His apartment had dildos stuck to the fridge. "For testing purposes," he said. Fascinating mind though -- went a mile a minute -- on how to fleece people. He plans to run the same scam again -- but this time using his own "coin" and blockchain.

2) December, 2019. The Hong Kong Bitcoin Bubble Bash! What an extravaganza. Met some amazing people. One guy from Saudi Arabia who's not allowed to drink alcohol back in the Arab Emirates -- so he travels to HK and gets absolutely plastered. Also met a hacker -- straight and true hacker; the guy bragged about ripping off an exchange for millions $$$$$ worth of crypto; I didn't believe him until he proved it (details revealed in the 2nd book). Anyway, we closed down the bar.

3) December/January 2019. Bitcoin going to $20,000 and the parabolic "to-the-moon" euphoria I felt -- we all felt -- watching our bitcoin rise and rise and rise. Watching that BTC rocketship felt like front row at a SpaceX launch going to Mars. Nothing seemed impossible. I thought I'd be travel-

ing the world on my 1 bitcoin forever. The price would keep rising and I'd keep cashing out smaller and smaller bits of BTC. A perpetual machine. Nothing could stop me. "I feel invisible!" I shouted -- feeling rich for the first time.

4) January, 2019 -- Myanmar. The whiplash from Bitcoins fall. All my shitty desires of traveling the world forever -- dashed as the price began to crater. But then it rose again. Oh, wait, no, it's falling again. Jesus Horatio Alger -- now it's back up! What a roller-coaster. What a ride.

5) January, 2019 -- seeing Myanmar. Used to be called Burma. Took a bus up to Old Bagan -- and for the first time in my life I fulfilled a childhood dream: exploring old temples like Indiana Jones. Loved those movies growing up. I'd dig up my neighbors sandbox in search of buried treasure. Then, in Old Bagan, I rented a rickety bicycle and rode around in dusty forests -- finding ancient temples and avoiding massive hornets nests. Fucking amazing. Spent Christmas there. Time of my life. Wished I wasn't alone though.

6) January, Bangkok. The story behind the title of this book -- Stolen Wallets: And Where to Buy Them -- comes from Bangkok.

The crypto community is strong here. Stayed with a guy who almost immediately after hearing my "1 Bitcoin around the world" plan decided to take me straight to the black markets of Bangkok. We met his friend who somehow has facilities to print the most stunning replica's of $10 bills -- which he then sells to locals who give them as "change" to unwitting tourists.
Bags full of fake Rolexes, obviously. Replica macbooks, iPhones, of course. BTC mining rigs too -- fake AF. And -- stolen wallets.

As promised. Hot to the touch. Freshly picked from the groves of tourist trees. Then there's the full moon party and New Year's party. My god. What a time. What. A. time.

Save that for the sequel though. Overall a wild ride. (Strippers in clubs had bitcoin QR codes tattooed on their thighs -- for tips. Two fingers away from their pussy. A Bitcoin QR code on the right thigh. An ethereum QR code on the left thigh).

7) Coinsbank Blockchain cruise 2018. The crazy tale of how I managed to get onboard that cruise ship. The massive parties on board. Meeting John McAfee. What a character. He ran a Bitcoin mining operation not far from Portland, Oregon -- up in Washington State. I asked him what he thought of Bitcoin mining's impact on the environment -- if it was bad for global warming. He said he'd keep mining Bitcoin until the last polar bear drowns. Damn. He knows how to stir the pot.

P.S. I met the girl again. Miss Satoshi Nakamoto. Things happened. Not those things though :/ Wait for the sequel. You'll be just as surprised as I was.

8) Bitcoin died. Or very nearly died. From rising to $20,000 and change -- it plummeted, absolutely nosedived ... to $6,000 something. Horrific. I drank myself stupid. That was Kuala Lumpur, Malaysia. I barely remember it. Horrible times. Horrible, nasty times.

9) February, 2019. Cambodia. The absolute hustle of Phnom Penh. Chinese investors clogging the casinos. Expats finding solitude and rebellion in this 21st Century's version of the Wild West.   I found a tiny dive bar that accepted BTC and ETH. I bought a "Bitcoiner's Delight" (A drink made of questionable bathtub gin).

Saw the infamous Killing Fields, S-21 Tuol Sleng torture

prison, the horrors of Pol Pot's Khmer Rouge. Cried for the first time in years. And later when the cab driver offered to take me to his 'good friend Jon's place' where I could 'shoot a bazooka' at a live tied-up cow so we could 'watch big explosion' -- I nearly punched him in the face. That's one messed up country #truth

10) After that things get beyond wild. Bitcoin keeps rolling around. Rising and sinking. My satoshi's dwindle. I still have months ahead of me.

I stick to the cheap countries: months in the Phillipians, India, Ethiopia, Egypt. It's not cheap enough. I can't find enough Couchsurfers to host me. I begin to rely on the crypto community.

End up finding it's cheaper to surf with crypto hosts in Europe: Poland, Germany, Switzerland, France, Belgium. I meet crypto guys who store their wallets on RFID chips implanted in their hands -- one guy pays at card swiping pads by waving his middle finger in front of it.

Some entrepreneurs are using blockchain to change the world -- others are using it for bigger and bigger exit scams -- and they're not afraid to brag about it ... getting rich off other people's backs. I lose touch with my parents. My satoshi's flow out of my wallet.

11) I meet her again. At my lowest point, in the worst country, with near nothing left to my name. I meet Miss Satoshi Nakamoto (real name in the sequel).

12) I'll stop spoiling it! Damn. Spoiling good stuff here. But I've left out the topshelf parts. The sleeping under a bridge, getting mugged, being lost, mistaken for a refuge and nearly deported, the ... alright, ALRIGHT, enough spoiling!

These are the tale tales you'll find in my sequel. Stay tuned. Watch for updates. Pester me with questions. Fill my inbox.

Still. Here you are with only half a book -- if that. And me going on about all crazy shit to follow. So, how will I make it up to you?

When the next half of the book comes out ... I'll give you the whole book as an ebook. You can have it as a PDF, ebook file, or other electronic means. Just email me after the 2nd half comes out (thebitcointravelers@gmail.com) and I'll do my damndest to send you a copy.

And don't forget about the Wordwallet prize. Hidden in this half of the book are 6 of the 12 words needed to unlock the BTC wallet with the bitcoin I've stashed in there.

Stay tuned to my Youtube channel (Aroundtheworldonabitcoin) for clues on what these words are and in which order they must be placed within the wallet to unlock it.

If you'd like to check the amount of BTC I put on the Wordwallet (and if me or anyone has put more on there) here's the address and QR code:

1PCG5muDkwXXkETCoibKztxgbf1aXYni1U

R.R. Hauxley

Also...

By way of thanks, for those of you who read to the end of the book, here's the first clue.

Word #3 in the wallet is .... Lottery

Lottery is the word.

It's number 3 of 12 in the Wordwallet. That's where it goes. In the 3rd position of the seed phrase. The rest (6 words out of the 12 word seed phrase) are somewhere in this book. Good luck.

Last word before I exit stage left...

The crypto community is, beyond a doubt, incredible.

I'd like to thank the people who's couches I crashed, who shared their music, gave me bus fare when I had no local fiat, inspired me to keep going despite all the times I wanted to give up, made soup out of goat testicales when I was sick, took me to their favorite dive bars, bailed me out of jail, made strange local foods their families used to make, taught me cuss words in their languages -- and how to ask for beer, bathrooms, and breadcrumbs(for a dish I wanted to cook), taught me the basics of coding (which I've since forgotten), confessed their fears to help me get over mine, and just .... Were human with me.

Thank you.

For those who feel so inclined ...

An address/QR code for donations:

Bitcoin Segwit address:
Bc1qft25lekzltghgwzx9ahemepknk78z2w24hv4zf

R.R. Hauxley

Ethereum:
0x7971502095Fca3D6A752196cb62634c426D156D7

Zcash:
t1Qs8qxSySeqWwvVyi9ueJKqWWcU5z8Dswr

Monero:

4GdoN7NCTi8a5gZug7PrwZNKjvHFmKeV11L6pNJPgj5QNEHs-
N6eeX3DaAQFwZ1ufD4LYCZKArktt113W7QjWvQ7CWBd-
P61ei4MCCkaN3cP

Printed in Great Britain
by Amazon